AF413117

Richwood Revisited

More Tales from the Historic Village

Dustin K. Lowe

Lake Baccarat Press
Richwood, Ohio

Published by Lake Baccarat Press
An imprint of Dustin Lowe Publishing

Images obtained with permission by Charles (Chuck) Barry and the Richwood-North Union Public Library

Manufactured in the United States of America

ISBN: 979-8-218-37396-2 (hardcover)

DEDICATED TO

My friends and family who encouraged me to continue
researching and learning about our interesting village.

CONTENTS

PREFACE

I have been fascinated about history since I started college in 2016. I went to The Ohio State University in Marion and graduated with a Bachelor's degree in English. I had thought extensively about majoring in history which was a personal passion of mine but really one of the only jobs you could get with this was teaching. Not only was I iffy on the whole teaching thing, but if I had to teach, I would've preferred the college level so that I could research what interested me. But, as you may or may not know, higher academia jobs are a very saturated field with very few positions available. So I chose English because I also love literature and it translates to a lot of different fields.

During college I would take a bunch of history electives and a few seminars on historical methodology used by past historians. We would learn things like examining how historians conceive of their object of study, how they use primary sources as a basis for their accounts, how they structure the narrative and analytic discussion of their topic, and what are the advantages and drawbacks of their various approaches. This is what got me into the world of historical academia.

In one of these classes, it was a requirement to get an internship and so I was able to volunteer at the Delaware Historical Society. The group there are a great bunch of people who take their history very seriously. I learned a lot in those few months such as processing donations, cataloging them on the software, researching various topics and writing articles for their newsletter. The internship, however, was cut short because of COVID-19. Prior to this I had also been working part time at the Richwood-North Union Public Library as a page.

During the pandemic, two of my coworkers had left the library to pursue other opportunities. It was at this time that I got promoted to assistant librarian. One of the things I had to think about was, apart from normal working duties, what I wanted to do in terms of off-desk projects. I decided on revamping the neglected local history room. The room had seen much better days and so I took upon the challenge of organizing it. I took what I learned during my internship and greatly improved the history room. I was able to basically establish a history department within the library.

During this time, I was able to get a few historical donations here and there which I cataloged and scanned online for public use. I also found myself surrounded by a ton of Richwood history. A lot of it was scattered around and written by various people that had previously researched what interested them. I took a lot of what I found plus my own research and wrote a book called *The Rich Woods of Union County: A Comprehensive History of Richwood, Ohio*. The subtitle, however, was a lie. As I continued my career, I found a lot more history that not a lot of people seemed to be aware of. And thus, this book was born. This is my attempt at a "sequel" to my original book. I hope this book will delight you with the rich and fascinating history that I have discovered in Richwood's nearly two centuries of existence.

Chapter 1

THE RICHWOOD TRI-COUNTY FAIR

Richwood has long been known for its horse racing with the founding of the Ohio Quarter Horse Association by W.P. Drake, M.D. and a long and successful business called Ken Davis & Sons which continues to provide farrier and horse equipment to most of central and eastern Ohio. The Richwood Tri-County Fair began in 1892 with a call for anyone interested in having a permanent ground where a fair can be held. In the Richwood Gazette on July 21, 1892, the editors had put this notice in the paper, "To all parties interested in Richwoods wellfare [sic] and the success of her Street Fairs due notice is given that a public meeting is called for this evening at eight o'clock at the mayor's office, this call is signed by James Huggert, Sec'y., and D.F. Parsons, Pres't. This meeting is called to feel the pulse of our citizens as to the advisability of securing permanent grounds where the fair can be held each year, either through purchase or lease. As this is the first meeting called to arrange for our Street Fair all are advised to be on hand, a full and free discussion is expected upon all points at issue. Don't fail to attend as it is of the utmost importance that this Fair matter should be attended to at once."

During the meeting, the success of former street fairs, which were held every year on Franklin Street, was talked over and the probable success of a fair held upon permanent grounds, with suitable buildings for all necessary purposes where a nominal admission fee would be charged, was discussed. It was decided that such a fair would be a grand success if all parties interested would take hold. A committee of three: John Ogan, P.K. Barnes and J.A. Huggert, were appointed to negotiate with M.W. Hill for his racetrack and to get an option on it. The property contained about thirty acres with a price of $4,500. The intention was to form a stock company of $6,000 in shares of $50, each. About one-third was guaranteed at the meeting. Those subscribing for the stock had a little more than two years to pay it in, namely, one-third in the next September, one-third in September 1893, and one-third in September 1894. Mr. Hill's proposition was to deed the property outright to the association, taking these notes in full for payment. He also would take stock equal in amount to any two subscribers. The committee was also authorized to canvass the county for subscriptions to the capital stock. All who had any interest in the success of Richwood, or the farmers of this vicinity were urged to call and put their names down for one or more shares.

With the plan successfully put through, Richwood had it's very first Tri-County Fair which was held on October 11, 12, 13, and 14, 1892. The fair was largely touted as a success. With the purchasing of Morris W. Hill's racetrack, the early Richwood Fair Association established a permanent exhibition in Richwood for all to enjoy. Enough interest was manifested at the first meeting to secure subscriptions to permit the

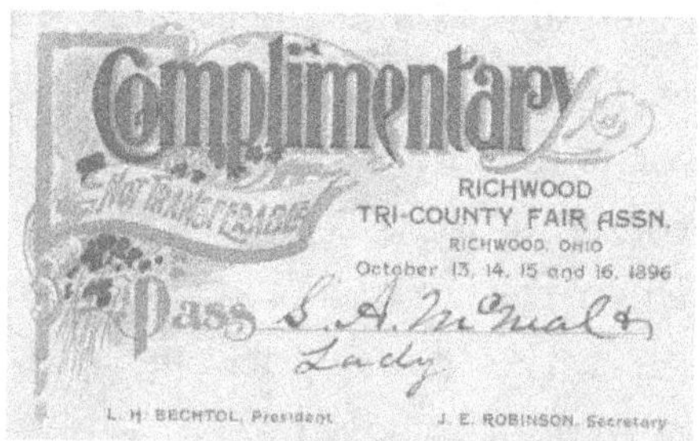

Richwood Fair pass from 1896. Courtesy of Richwood-North Union Public Library. Via Ohio Memory.

buying of the grounds and putting them in proper shape. This also allowed the association when opening to be free from debt. In fact, more people subscribed since the purchase to allow an additional five more acres, giving them an extra outlet on another road. As the grounds now stood, there was about thirty-five acres, which had cost the Association about $5,100.

Once they secured the property, the Association had improved the track, put up additional stalls, new pens, a dining hall, and a large fine arts hall. A grandstand had been erected by private parties which reverted to the Association in five years, or they could buy it at the end of two years. It was late when the Association got on its feet and began spreading the news about the fair, however, each and every moment was made to count. The Board's genial Secretary, Mr. James A. Huggert, was mentioned in the Gazette for the amount of work he put into getting the fair started in such a short time. The weather was reported to have been perfect throughout the week and one could easily detect a smile of satisfaction hovering over the massive brows of stockholders and the

An advertisement of the first tri-county fair held in Richwood in 1892. Via Richwood Gazette, Sept. 22, 1892.

Board.

During the fair a Mrs. Roberts, of south Prospect, sent a mammoth yam into the fair, measuring 12 inches long and 6 in diameter and weighing 7 lbs. A private display of carriages, buggies, road carts, etc., by two different firms, was on display for all to see. Also on display were vegetables, pumpkins, fruits and a wide range of canned and preserved fruits and berries. The Fine Arts Hall was too small for the exhibits offered and it was requested that it should be enlarged for next year or used for other purposes and another one be built. Horses were well represented as were cattle, sheep, and poultry. It was reported that a few exhibitors from neighboring towns came here with the intention of running the fair, laying down the law to the judge and doing what they wanted. However, they struck a snag in the judge and went off with their tail between their legs. The Gazette indicated that it was a pleasure to learn that the Board upheld the judge. Machinery wasn't represented because of such short notice.

Only one accident occurred, and it was regretted by the Board and the entire community. The driver of H.B.M., Lou Seeseholtz, of Johnstown, Ohio, put an extra strain upon the reins and broke them into two pieces. This allowed his horse to run into another, precipitating him headlong onto the track. Fortunately, he was far enough removed so that he was out of the way of the other horses, receiving a broken ankle and some very bad bruises. Dr. Duke was called who attended him, making Mr. Seeseholtz as comfortable as possible under the circumstances. It was stated as remarkable to see the driverless horse make a complete circuit and a half of the track without accident, coming in first, although under the rules he could not be awarded the beat.

In October 1900, the ninth annual fair of the Richwood Tri-County Fair held its biggest one yet with a record breaking ten thousand people in attendance (as claimed by the Richwood Gazette). The entries in the horse, cattle, sheep, hog, poultry, and fine art departments exceeded anything ever before in Richwood, while the farm products looked just as good as the best county fair in the state of Ohio. Over fifty head of horses were entered in the trotting and pacing races, and a big string of runners were on hand in the racehorse events. The horses had visited the Richwood Fair from four states: Ohio, Indiana, Pennsylvania, and Illinois. The biggest, and most expensive attraction was Cook's Royal Hippodrome which carried 16 thoroughbred horses, dogs, and chariots. They gave exciting exhibitions including standing jockey races, Roman standing races, running tandem races, hurdle races, chariot races, hounds vs horse bucking horses, two mile race, changing mounts each half mile, and a grand steeple chase besides other specialties too numerous to describe. After each heat was decided, the track would be cleared, and the exhibitions would begin.

The total receipts for the three days exceeded those of last years, which was then considered the largest in the history of the association. The expenses that year were considerably more than previous years on account of the advanced price of labor which the association was compelled to employ, however, enough money was made to pay off all the indebtedness and still have a nest egg for next year. The results of the different races are on the next page.

RESULT OF THE DIFFERENT RACES.

Wednesday, October 10.

2:40 Trot—Purse $200.

Maggie V	1	5	1	1
Banister Wilkes	5	1	3	2
Alec	2	2	5	4
Dr. Strong	3	3	2	5
Pete W	4	4	4	3

Time—2:24¼, 2:25¼, 2:24¼, 2:21¼.

2:20 Pace—Purse $200.

Topsy R	1	1	1
Dr. Douglas	3	2	4
Lady Hinsley	2	6	5
Jimmie R	9	12	2
Legal Hal	4	4	3
Atlanta B	5	3	11
O K	6	5	12
Coasta	7	7	8
Mirtes French	8	10	10
So Sure	11	9	6
Miss Francis	10	11	9
Brother Jonathan	12	8	7

Time—2:16¼, 2:16¼, 2:18¼.

Thursday, October 11.

2:35 Pace—Purse $200.

St. Patrick's Bell	1	1	1
Cevers	2	2	2
Rosco G	dis		

Time—2:21, 2:26, 2:22¼.

Free-for-all Trot—Purse $250.

Bertha Lee	1	1	1
Wheaton Boy	2	2	3
Crystal Rock	3	3	2

Time—2:21, 2:21, 2:19¼.

Running, 4½ furlongs, heats—Purse $100.

Rouble, b g, by Imp. Rossington	2	1	1
Duce, ch s, by Teuton	2	2	2
Mollie Again, b m, by Once Again	3	3	
Vita, br m, by Fordam	4	4	

Time—57¼, 56½, 57¾.

Friday, October 12.

2:23 Trot—Purse $200.

Maggie V	2	2	1	1	1
Lady Clark	1	1	2	2	2
Merry Mark	4	3	3	3	3
Zip	3dr				

Time—2:21¼, 2:25, 2:19¼, 2:20¼, 2:19¾.

Free-for-all Pace—Purse $250.

Circle	1	1	1
Frank Ryedike	2	2	3
Gypsy Red	3	3	2

Time—2:11¼, 2:11¼, 2:12.

Running, 6 furlongs, heats—Purse $130.

Rouble, b g, by Imp. Rossington	1	1
Darius, br g, by Emperor	2	2
Incidental b g, by Protection	5	3
Duce, ch s, by Teuton	3	4
Mollie Again b m, by Once Again	4	5

Time—1:17¼, 1:17¾.

Results of the horse races held at the fair from October 10-12, 1900. Via Richwood Gazette, Oct. 18, 1900.

Chapter 2

PROHIBITION IN RICHWOOD

The Prohibition Movement began following the more moderate Temperance Movement after the American Civil War had ended. The Temperance Movement encouraged people to abstain from selling or drinking alcohol. It wasn't about prohibition, that is, passing laws that compelled people to behave in a particular way. Instead, it was a movement grounded in moral persuasion; by changing individual behavior by influencing. Temperance supporters believed that freedom meant something very particular. Freedom meant freedom from addictive vices and bad habits and undermines self-discipline, self-improvement, and respectability. Today we tend to see the consumption of alcohol less as a bad habit that oppresses individuals but rather as a consumer choice. It doesn't matter what you choose, only that **you** choose. For Temperance Crusaders, however, abstaining from alcohol was a liberating act; it was an act that demonstrated you could govern yourself.

The Temperance Movement resonated with many Ohioans. One possible reason is that Ohioans had experienced intense urbanization, industrialization and emigration. Its cities struggled

The Temperance Movement was referred to as the "Woman's Holy War." Lithograph by Currier & Ives, c. 1874.

with urban squalor, economic exploitation and poverty. Migration and emigration to this world was alienating. Most new Ohioans had lived as their ancestors had lived for countless centuries. The modern world of anonymous cities, brutal factories and dense city living was stressful and challenged the stability of family life.

The aftereffects of the American Civil War also played a part. After the war, there was a noticeable increase in alcohol consumption. In the small town of Washington Courthouse, for example, the number of saloon keepers expanded from zero in 1860 to eight in 1870 all for about 2,000 residents. Clearly, the aftershocks of war added to the stress of a state undergoing rapid transformation. Alcohol seemed to offer a salve against social change and post-traumatic stress.

Over the course of 1873 to 1874, there were Temperance Crusades in 31 states and territories involving some 54 thousand women; 60% of those women protested in Ohio. They marched down Main streets, they drafted petitions, they got pledges from people to stop drinking, they picketed saloons by singing hymns at the door as men passed in and out. Often, they were harassed, jostled by men, spat upon, drenched in old beer and dirty water. In Ohio alone, there were 300 Crusades in 200 different places. The women of Washington courthouse, for example, had great success as they managed to persuade the owners of all of the bars to shut down.

The Temperance Movement was later eclipsed by the Prohibition Movement which compelled people to stop drinking. That movement was also set in Ohio and it was led by the Anti-Saloon League which was founded in Oberlin, Ohio in 1893 and relocated to Westerville in 1909. This movement, unlike the Temperance Movement, was led mainly by men. They focused their efforts on the complete abolition of the sale of alcohol through outlets such as saloons. The organization was effective and was able to build off of the Temperance Movement. But, more than any other organization, they helped persuade America to amend the constitution, ratifying the 18th amendment in 1919 to outlaw the manufacture and distribution of alcohol. An important fact to note here is that it wasn't illegal to drink alcohol, just creating and selling it.

By 1908, there were a total of fifteen various saloons in Union County; eight in Marysville, three in Richwood, three at Milford Center and one in Magnetic Springs. A petition containing the signatures of 3412 voters was filed on September 9th, 1908 with the Common Pleas Judge in Marysville. The petition called for a special election on October 5th under the Rose Bill. The Rose Bill, also called the Rose Law, allowed individual communities to put Prohibition issues on their local ballots. If a majority of residents voted in favor of the issue, then saloons could not operate in the community. Many Ohio towns and cities took advantage of the Rose Law to ban the sale of alcohol in their communities. The Union County Board of Elections were then ordered to have ballots printed for a special election.

The Richwood Gazette posted an article in the paper in September titled, "Attention Farmers and Land Owners: Your vote is Important. Carefully examine the following figures from the State Auditor's Reports for 1907 then decide for yourself how you honestly think you should cast your ballot." The article lists the following facts and figures taken from the Ohio Auditor of State's Report of 1907:

1- By levying a state tax of 1.345 mills on all tangible property, the state of Ohio derived...$3,012,115.05

2- The state received from the liquor tax...$2,749,750.99

3- The state received from all other sources of revenue...$780,732.70

Total revenue of the state in 1907...$6,542,598.74

The Gazette then pointed out that if the saloons in Ohio were voted out of existence, at least $2,749,750.99 in revenue of the state would be destroyed. This revenue is 91.5 per cent of the total amount ($3,012,115.05) the state raised by direct taxation by a state levy of 1,345 mills. "This revenue must be made from some other source, and that source will be by direct taxation on your farm, your real estate, and your house, for this class of property is sure to bear the brunt of the inevitable increased taxation." The liquor tax paid for 42% of the running expenses of the state. The Gazette warned that the state tax rate would double to compensate for the loss of revenue. They later state, "Do not be led astray by fanatical and emotional appeals from the non-taxpaying Anti-Saloon League and its salaried itinerant agitators."[1]

The Richwood Gazette publishes an article a week later exposing the "false statements" made by the Anti-Saloon League. The paper claims that the organization lies about a reduction in taxes that follows wherever the income from the liquor tax is wiped out. "This on its very face sound very paradoxical." They later point out that, "It stands to reason that when you destroy one source of income, the difference must be made up somewhere else."[2] The organization likes to point to Washington Courthouse as a good example of this. When called upon to explain this strange condition, they point out that the town didn't need as many policemen which made up the loss of the liquor tax. The Gazette delves into this by providing the expenses paid to police in the town:

	1904	1905	1906	1907
Paid for police duty	$2887.00	$3050.00	$1506.00	$1854.00
Received from liquor tax	$1902.05	$1806.07	$223.62	________

It should be added that Washington Courthouse had four policemen while the town was "wet," and that when the revenue from the liquor tax was cut off, expenses had to be curtailed so that in May, 1906, and for the balance of that year there was only one regular policeman on the pay roll of the town. More policeman were needed as shown by the increase in 1907's numbers. However, the biggest reduction in funding was for public services such as street repairs, street cleaning, sewage, public lighting, ect. In 1905, the public services fund in the town was 7.75 mills. In 1908, that had been reduced to 6 mills. As used in property tax, 1 mill is equal to $1 in property tax levied per $1,000 of a property's assessed value. It can therefore be seen that a loss in the liquor tax actually did require the town to make up the difference in other ways despite not raising the taxes on residents.

Despite the Gazette's constant insistence otherwise, Union County had overwhelmingly voted "dry." By a decisive majority of 1799, the voters of Union County, regardless of politics, had decided that they disproved of the continuation of saloons. Reportedly, many men who were addicted to alcohol also voted dry to try to kick the habit. The total number of votes cast in the county was 5721, the largest voting number in the history of the county at the time. Of this number, the drys voted 3738 and the wets 1935. The drys won every municipality and township in the county except for Darby township which gave wets the majority by a total of 23 votes. A complete tally of the votes in all townships in Union County follows:

Voting Precincts	Drys	Wets
Allen	180	38
Claiborne, N.	116	39
Claiborne, S.	142	41
Richwood, N.	186	77
Richwood, S.	138	77
Darby	81	141
Unionville Center	56	29
Dover	165	57
Jackson	199	43
Jerome, E.	81	41
Jerome, W.	90	52
Plain City	101	37
Leesburg, E.	96	24
Leesburg, W.	107	52
Magnetic Springs	82	15
Liberty	264	96
Millcreek	98	56
Paris, E.	39	71
Paris, W.	114	46
Marysville, 1st w.	92	135
Marysville, 2nd w.	107	132
Marysville, 3rd w.	109	83
Marysville, 4th w.	173	192
Taylor	180	75
Union, N.	66	73
Union, S.	73	47
Milford Center	114	98
Washington	148	105
York	378	53
Total vote	3734	1935
Dry majority	1799	

Results of the special election which resulted in the closing of saloons that served alcohol in Union County in 1908. Via Richwood Gazette, Oct. 8, 1908.

As a result of the election, all fifteen saloons in Union County were forced to close. The Rose local option law went into effect on November 4th, 1908 at 9:30 pm. Saturday evening on October 31, P.J. Speyer closed the doors to his saloon for good, having sold all his stock, and expressed interest in converting his building to a restaurant and pool hall. The two other bars in Richwood, owned by Carl Allgower and Ira Donahoe, were closed on November 4th at the same time that the law went into effect.

The town of Kenton had also voted dry around the same year. According to a discovery reported by a visitor from Bellefontaine, they started selling whiskey in oranges. "'Give me two oranges,' said the Bellefontaine visitor, as he threw down a silver dollar. They were carefully handed out accompanied by a wink from the dealer. The Bellefontaine man examined them before asking for change, and found inside of each orange a tin circular flask containing whisky. The purchaser of the oranges did not ask for change."[3]

Despite the prohibition of alcohol taking effect, many people were still able to get their fix one way or another. Some stores had underground bars which served alcohol illegally and others attempted to make alcohol themselves which caused many people to get sick. Bootleg alcohol was often of lesser quality and sometimes even dangerous. On average, 1,000 Americans died every year during Prohibition from the effects of drinking tainted liquor.

A man by the name of Ogan was voted as Mayor of Richwood on the first day of the year in 1910 and promised many reforms. The first thing he did was rearrange the mayor's office and made a much-needed cleaning of the entire premises. He then called all members of the new council and

A whiskey advertisement appearing in the Richwood Gazette in 1913, five years after Union County had voted dry. Whiskey was often sold for "medicinal" purposes during the Prohibition Era. Via Richwood Gazette, Oct. 2, 1913.

talked over many things which might be improved upon in the town. One of the things talked about at this conference was the enforcement of the curfew ordinance which was passed by the council a few years prior. It was enforced for a time and was the means of keeping many children off the streets during the night unless accompanied by a parent or guardian. It was decided to enforce this curfew again and on the first night of the new year, Marshal Sloop cleared the streets of the usual gang of children who had been in the habit of loitering in the streets late at night.

The "bootlegger" problem also came up for discussion and it was of the council's opinion that the "bootlegger" and "common drunks" who make it a point to loiter around the corners and alleys of Richwood be made to obey to ordinances of the town and laws of Ohio. Since Richwood and Union County voted the town "dry" in 1908, and thereby imposed an extra tax of $1500 per annum upon the taxpayers of Richwood, it was of the opinion that as long as the town remains "dry" in name, it should also be "dry" in reality.

On April 9, 1910, a twenty-two-year-old man by the name of Omer DeGood was arrested that morning while on his way to the fairgrounds with a basket filled with whiskey and beer. He was locked up in the village prison and a search and seizure warrant sworn out by Marshal Sloop who, together with Deputy Marshal Aller, went to the home of the parents of Mr. DeGood who resided on North Franklin Street. They succeeded in finding many empty bottles of whiskey and jugs. The officers hauled the goods off to the mayor's office in grocery carts.

That evening, DeGood was given a preliminary hearing before Mayor Ogan and plead not guilty to bootlegging and was placed under $300 bond. Failing to come up with the required bond, he was again placed in the village prison to wait until Tuesday morning for a hearing. When he appeared before the hearing that morning, he again plead not guilty. In the meantime, Marshal Sloop and others had done what they could to provide direct evidence where it could be proven that Mr. DeGood violated the Rose Law. Although this was impossible to prove, the next best thing for the officers to do was to banish the young man from the town. There were many complaints before this incident against his conduct. He agreed to this arrangement and signed an article stating that he was not to return to Richwood. The Richwood Gazette points out that, "The Rose law is a failure in many respects and has not accomplished much good in Union County, which was voted dry by a big majority. Since its passage it is said by those in a position to know that there is as much, if not more, whisky consumed than before the saloons were voted out. They say it has changed many moderate beer drinkers to consumers of whiskey and other stimulants detrimental to the general health."[4]

The Richwood Gazette's problems with Prohibition continued with an article on July 14, 1910, in which they accuse the Anti-Saloon League of not wanting to rid Columbus of their saloons. "If the Anti-Saloon League is so anxious to rid Ohio of the liquor traffic why not begin operations right at home? Directly under the noses of the officers of the League in Columbus, are about three hundred saloons. Why not clean them out first? They know full well these saloons are the source of supply for numerous 'dry' counties in central Ohio and that they attract thousands of people to Columbus every week. Is it possible the League wants to see Columbus 'wet' and surrounding towns 'dry' in order to help Columbus financially? It looks very much as if this was the case."[5]

Things further worsened for Richwood when, in December of 1911, the village council was forced to borrow $300 to pay the salaries of village officials. Up until the past three years, Richwood had always had from $3,000 to $5,000 on deposit in the local banks. After the county voted dry in 1908, however, the village was cut short $1,500 a year or a total of $4,500 for the three years, which was the cause of the deficiency in the treasury. Richwood was now in the financial predicament that many, three years ago, foreseen the village would reach. Richwood was not alone in this situation either. Both Milford Center and Marysville had been cut short from $1,500 to $5,000 per annum by the county voting dry.

The Rose law was later modified in 1910, referred to as the Beal law, to allow individual towns and municipalities such as Richwood or Marysville to vote on whether they wanted to remain dry with the county or choose to go wet. The towns of Marion and Prospect did just that. The citizens of Prospect voted under the Beal law and voted wet by a majority of 19 votes. The total votes cast was 304 with 142 voting dry while 161 voted wet. The remaining one vote was illegal. At the county level, Marion County voted dry by a majority of 37 in 1911. Soon afterward, Marion decided to continue their saloon business in the town. Prospect, being between the wet towns of Columbus and Marion and not wanting to lose out on revenue, decided to also continue selling alcohol. They would later vote dry on April 3, 1919 with the resulting closure of the saloon operated by Schelgel and Speyer.

By 1914, a total of 45 counties were considered dry in the state of Ohio. An election was held in Ohio on November 3, 1914. Four different amendments were on the ballot. Amendment 1 provided home rule on alcohol which allowed the citizens of local municipalities and townships the right to decide, without state intervention, if they wanted to sell alcohol or not. Amendment 2 provided limitation on tax rate and property classification. Amendment 3 provided voting rights for women. Amendment 4 would enact a prohibition on the sale of alcohol as beverages in the state of Ohio. Amendment 1 was the only one on the ballot that passed. The following is an advertisement in the Richwood Gazette paid for by the Anti-Saloon League who supported Prohibition:

VOTE "NO" ON HOME RULE
VOTE "YES" ON PROHIBITION

Ask the first ten Mothers you meet if they would vote for the saloon—and govern yourself accordingly.

The man who drinks is the First Man to be laid off and the Last Man to be taken on. Think it over.

A traffic that will not be controlled must be prohibited.

Sample Official Ballot Marked to Vote Against Brewers' Home Rule Proposal and for State Prohibition

		Proposed Amendments to Constitution
	YES	ARTICLE XV. Sec. 9a
X	NO	Home rule on the subject of intoxicating liquors.
	YES	ARTICLE XII. Sec. 1 and 2. Limitation on the tax rate and for the classification of property for purposes of taxation.
	NO	
	YES	ARTICLE V. Sec. 1.
	NO	To extend the suffrage to women.
X	YES	ARTICLE XV. Sec. 9. Prohibition of the sale, manufacture for sale and importation for sale of intoxicating liquor as a beverage.
	NO	

Here is the official amendment ballot. It is the same size as the ballot the judges will hand you at the booth on election day and in all respects it is a counterpart of the ballot you will vote, except, of course, the ballot given you in the booth will not have any cross marks on it. The ballot as marked above is marked for a vote against the brewers' home rule amendment and for the state Prohibition amendment.

Cut this ballot out, get acquainted with the arrangement of the several proposals, and how to mark it to register your vote against the home rule amendment and for the Prohibition amendment.

The proposed amendments will be on a ballot by themselves and in the order shown in the sample ballot, with the titles as here given. Except, of course, there will be no cross mark on the ballot the election judges will give you.

It will be seen by the cross marks on this sample ballot that temperance voters in order to make their votes effective must vote "No" on the home rule proposed and "Yes" on the Prohibition proposal.—Adv.

An advertisement in the Richwood Gazette published before the election on November 3, 1914. It encouraged voters to support Prohibition, which banned the sale of alcohol, and to oppose the Home Rule Amendment, which would give more power to local governments. Via Richwood Gazette, Oct. 22, 1914.

In terms of results for political office, Warren G. Harding was elected to the United States Senate with Frank B. Willis being elected as Ohio Governor. The state legislature was comprised of mostly Republicans. The home rule amendment was later taken to the Ohio Supreme Court after a case was brought in by Franklin County Common Pleas Court by Charles S. Hockett, a piano dealer from Bellefontaine. He alleged that this amendment violated the general welfare provision of the federal constitution and that an attempt was being made to divest the people of certain rights of which they, themselves, could not put aside. The case was pressed for counsel by the Anti-Saloon League. It was appealed and the Supreme Court held that the amendment was in fact valid.

The state liquor licensing board announced in 1915 that the thirty-one counties which will get county license boards under the home rule amendment will have a total of 493 saloons (versus 823 saloons in those counties in 1908, before the votes to dry). Union county had a total of 9 saloons open. The Anti-Saloon League continued their fight to repeal the Home Rule Amendment and aimed to pass a state-wide prohibition of alcohol.

Residents in Claibourne Township, outside of Richwood, quietly circulated a petition to hold a vote on June 23, 1917 to decide if the township should permit saloons to start selling alcohol again. A similar petition and subsequent vote was presented to the citizens of Richwood in January of 1915 and was not passed. In fact, the election was taken to the Supreme Court of Ohio. The drys won by a majority of one vote since a couple votes on both sides of the issue were marked as invalid. The courts decided in favor of the drys and Richwood remained as such. Those who supported the prohibition of alcohol were fearful of saloons being operated outside the city limits which is exactly what a few citizens of Claibourne Township tried to do. The petition filed contained names in excess of the number required by law. Under the home rule amendment, only those who resided in Claibourne Township and outside the city limits of Richwood were permitted to vote on the resolution. Dry voters outnumbered the wets ten to one and the resolution was not passed.

As the first World War raged, the Unites States Congress passed the temporary Wartime Prohibition Act, which banned the sale of alcoholic beverages having an alcohol content of greater than 1.28%. This act, which had been intended to save grain for the war effort, was passed after the armistice ending World War I was signed on November 11, 1918. The Wartime Prohibition Act took effect June 30, 1919, with July 1, 1919 becoming known as the "Thirsty First." The U.S. Senate proposed the Eighteenth Amendment on December 18, 1917. On October 28, 1919, Congress passed enabling legislation, known as the Volstead Act, to enforce the Eighteenth Amendment when it went into effect in 1920. Upon being approved by a 36th state (Ohio being one of them) on January 16, 1919, the amendment was ratified as a part of the Constitution. By the terms of the amendment, the country went dry one year later, on January 17, 1920 when the Volstead Act went into effect. A total of 1,520 Federal Prohibition agents were tasked with enforcement.

P.J. Speyer's Cafe located on North Franklin Street in Richwood circa 1900. The cafe was one of two other establishments in Richwood that were forced to stop selling alcohol when the Rose Law was enacted in Union County in 1908. Photo courtesy of Chuck Barry.

Doctors were able to prescribe medicinal alcohol for their patients. After just six months of prohibition, over 15,000 doctors and 57,000 pharmacists received licenses to prescribe or sell medicinal alcohol. A majority of U.S. citizens obeyed the law, although some states like Maryland and New York refused prohibition. Enforcement of the amendment lacked a centralized authority. Many churches formed vigilante groups to enforce it along with organizations such as the Ku Klux Klan, although it was poorly organized and seldom had any impact. As the Great Depression hit in 1929, state governments needed the tax revenue that alcohol sales generated. When Franklin Roosevelt was elected in 1932, he strongly urged the repeal of Prohibition. The Eighteenth Amendment was officially repealed on December 5, 1933 with the ratification of the Twenty-first Amendment to the U.S. Constitution. The Twenty-first Amendment didn't prevent states and municipalities from banning or restricting alcohol thereby allowing local control of alcohol. With the Amendment gone, the country was effectively half wet and half dry.

In November 1933, Richwood held an election to vote on the mayoral race. Included on the ballot was an option to repeal the ban on the sale of liquor in Richwood. 619 total votes were against the repeal with 487 votes for. Richwood continued to remain dry even after local elections in 1937 and in 1941 where the citizens of Richwood once again voted against the sale of liquor in Richwood by a nice majority. The elections in 1945 onward included no mention of the prohibition of liquor.

With the end of the Prohibition Amendment, one thing became pretty clear. By prohibiting these sales, the state of Ohio as well as the United States economy would see large losses directly and indirectly from alcohol sales. Supporters of the prohibition expected an increase in the sales of other products such as other beverages like juice and soda to replace the money made from alcohol sales, but this could not be further from reality. The Bureau of Internal

Revenue estimated that the prohibition caused the shutdown of over 200 distilleries, a thousand breweries, and over 170,000 liquor stores. Organized criminal organizations saw this as an opportunity to make a lot of cash. Enforcement of the ban had to be paid for to fight the war against both alcohol and crime. The amount of money used to enforce prohibition started at 6.3 million in 1921 and rose to 13.4 million in 1930, almost double the original amount.

Chapter 3

HALLOWEEN IN RICHWOOD

The following was written in the Richwood Gazette in October of 1874, "On the 31st of this month occurs what is known as All Hallow Eve, or Halloween. Of all the quaint superstitions that have been handed down to us, there are none that have taken a deeper hold upon the popular imagination than the observance of this event. The leading belief in regard to the Halloween is that of all others, it is the time when spirits, both of the visible and invisible world walk abroad and can be invoked by human powers for the purpose of revealing the mysterious future, and spirits may be ailed from the vasty deep at will."[6]

Halloween didn't start out as kids dressing up and going door to door for candy. That is a fairly recent phenomenon. Halloween originally began as a way for kids to play practical jokes and cause mischief. In Richwood in the late 1800s, kids would throw cabbages at people's property and move objects in the road, obstructing traffic. One particular story shows the dangers of doing so, "That evening above all others in the year when the spirit of deviltry seems to predominate in all young people and prompt them to do things of which they are frequently much ashamed the next day, and which usually gets them into any amount of trouble is the holiday, or rather time of Halloween. The meaning of the day or why it is celebrated in the maner [sic] in which young America celebrates it, none can tell exactly although there are numbers of reasons given, and some of them may be correct, but we are of the opinion it was invented especially for everyone to give vent to all the deviltry which has lain half dormant within them all year, and to say that it is usually given good lengths of rope would be putting it mildly.

This photo was taken in the attic of what is now Stofcheck-Ballinger Funeral Home circa 1920. It was common around this time for teachers to hold Halloween parties after school for their class. Photo courtesy of Chuck Barry.

"The Richwood youths played the same old trick of stealing gates, throwing cabbage, corn, beans, etc., against the windows of business places and residences, pulling wagons and buggies onto the sidewalks and putting them in front of business places, etc., etc. To the early riser the streets presented an appearance of having been passed over by a cyclone on Sunday morning. But the spirit of misplacing things went too far with James Kinnear and Ellis Parish who placed an old buckboard on the Erie track near Beem's mill. It was evidently placed there to be struck by the express train from the east, but it being late the obstruction was hit by a through freight train coming from the west. The headlight was badly broken and the light extinguished, while the buckboard was reduced to fragments and the train compelled to go to Marion without the light which reveals to the engineer all dangerous places in the road, and without which he is, while running his train, like a man 'taking a leap in the dark.'

"The fact was communicated to Marshal Cunningham who after a little detective work landed the above-named youths behind the bars on Sunday. Both confessed the crime and were placed under $500 bonds on Monday morning and in default of bail were on the same morning taken to jail at Marysville and at the next term of court will no doubt receive the limit of the law. If they do hot they richly deserve such. The offense is a penitentiary one. The boys are both toughs having been in other devilment.

"Not long since a corn cultivator belonging to George Handley was badly broken up and a boy fined, but Ellis Parish owned up to having a hand in its destruction, while on the way to jail. Some of his father's sheep have at times disappeared and the carcasses were found buried. He is a son of Daniel Parish, a good farmer and a splendid gentleman, whose Military career is an honorable one and who is a member of the Livingston Post, and is much grieved at the actions of his son, who with such a father should be a gentleman. His parents, as well as those of Kinnear, have our sympathy."[7] Daniel Parish later published a notice in the Gazette, stating that he had never found the carcass of a sheep buried at his farm and hadn't owned sheep for at least four years.

In 1892, the Richwood Gazette's large bulletin board, which weighed 300 pounds and was located just outside the Gazette office, was later found adorning a hay stack on the outskirts of town. The paper claimed they knew the names of half the kids who did it and prompted them to return it back the way it was before the sheriff gets involved. Other aftermath included country roads being blocked by fences, corn stalks being rooted from fields and planted in people's yards, and various remains of cabbage scattered across people's properties.

Halloween parties were also held and were well attended by young people. Activities like bobbing for apples and pumpkin carving was still very prevalent. It wasn't until the 1930s when children were given everything from homemade cookies and pieces of cake to fruit, nuts, coins and toys. In the 1950s, candy manufacturers began to get in on the act and promote their products for Halloween, and as trick-or-treating became more popular, candy was increasingly regarded as an affordable, convenient offering. It wasn't until the 1970s, though, that wrapped, factory-made candy was viewed as the only acceptable thing to hand out to all the little ghosts and goblins that showed up on people's doorsteps. A key reason for this was safety, as parents feared that real-life boogeymen might tamper with goodies that weren't store-bought and sealed.

Chapter 4

RICHWOOD PRESBYTERIAN CHURCH

Richwood is no stranger to the Christian faith. Many different churches and denominations have appeared throughout the years. In fact, a reverend by the name of Barkdull complained in 1888 that Richwood had too many church denominations. At that time, Richwood had 8 various congregations; The M.E., M.P., Presbyterian, two Baptist congregations, two Disciple, and the Adventist. The Rev.'s idea was to unite the various churches so that there would be greater unity.

Richwood and York Township (5 miles west of Richwood) both had Presbyterian churches at one point in its history. The Richwood Presbyterian Church was organized in 1874. The York Presbyterian Church was known to have been even older. The church was organized in 1839 with Andrew McNeil, father of Samuel McNeil, being one of its Ruling Elders. Andrew was regarded as one of the early settlers of Union County and York Township.

The Presbyterian Church in Richwood began with preaching services in Court's Hall by Rev. D.D. Waugh of Marion, Ohio starting on June 19th, 1874. The committee on church organization met on June 20th and organized and elected the proper officers. The committee consisted of Rev. D.D. Waugh, Rev. W.G. March, Rev. Henry Shedd, and Elder McNeil. Seventeen members constituted the organization of the church with a number of memberships added afterwards. Later that day, a session was started to receive members and attended to miscellaneous business. Preaching was done on Sunday mornings and evenings by Rev. Waugh.

A postcard stamped November 23, 1908 which displays the Richwood Presbyterian Church on the front. Correspondence on the back was to a Mr. Orville Richolson in Rockford, Ill. Courtesy of Richwood-North Union Public Library. Via Ohio Memory.

Members of the church continued to meet at Court's Hall, a large meeting hall that was located in Richwood. A year later, they moved to a new hall located on the second story above a clothing store named Burgner & Co. on Franklin St. where the current Richwood Bank building now stands. The building thankfully wasn't harmed by the fire of 1875. The room was originally occupied by a physician and surgeon by the name of Dr. P.H. Bauer before the congregation moved in. This hall was later referred to as the Presbyterian Hall. The Gazette had this to say about the church, "The services at the Presbyterian Church on Friday, Saturday and Sunday last, were interesting and well attended. Rev. J.A. McGaw, of Urbana, and Rev. D.D. Waugh, of Marion, were in attendance. Both are able ministers. The pastor, Charles S. Wood, feels greatly encouraged with their prospects, and feels confident of building up a thriving church. Quite a number of additions were made to the church on Sunday. They will organize their Sunday School shortly. Their hall is very elegantly and comfortably finished and [so] far they are clear of debt. Undoubtedly, they will prosper."[8]

The average attendance of the church was about 60 by the 1880s. On February 19, 1885, a Martha Washington Tea Party was held at the Presbyterian Hall. Supper was served to all who attended. The Martha Washington table was full of food from the olden days with old cutlery and candles served as lights. Admittance was 10 cents per person. George and Martha Washington and their friends appeared in costume to greet all guests. While Martha had a gracious smile and courtly bowed for each of her guests, George presided at the head of the table in silence and was very attentive in helping his guests to his or her choice of food. At the oyster table, various oysters were served in every style. Also served was pork and beans, roasted turkey, dried fruit, country-made bread, chicken salad, cold meats, coffee, cake, and tea. Many other people were dressed in revolutionary era clothing with powered hair and wigs. The church raised about $75 for the whole affair.

The congregation continued meeting at the Presbyterian Hall for numerous years until they felt that having a dedicated church building would be very beneficial. A committee of the Presbyterian congregation canvassed the town of Richwood for a few days in June of 1888. They sought subscriptions to help aid them of building a church building. The response was very gracious and work soon began on a new building. The Richwood Gazette commended the committee for serving home interests by hiring local contractors and using local labor rather than an outside contractor. The committee consisted of John Landon, Milton Shipley, Josiah Shipley, J.L. Horn, James Edelman, and Wesley Tallman. They purchased a property of James Wilcox, on the corner of Blagrove and Clinton streets for $1,400 in March. The building began to take shape in September,

1888.

On September 27, 1888, H.L. Clark, a local marble dealer, presented the to the building committee a marble tablet to place in front of the church building once finished. It had upon the slab in raised letters, "Presbyterian Church, A.D. 1888." The building was finished in January of 1889 with the dedication of the building being held on Sunday morning, January 20. A sermon was preached by Rev. A.D. Hawn of Delaware. He had this to say during the ceremony:

"The church may not fit a man for heaven, but it makes him more decent and prosperous in this world."[9]

—Rev. Hawn

The Presbyterian choir of Marysville provided music while Mrs. Rev. Ferguson presided at the organ. On the wall, in the rear of the pulpit, hung a banner in letters of gold which read, "Go up to the mountain and bring wood and build the house, and I will take pleasure in it and will be glorified, saith the Lord. Haggai 1:8". There is some history connected with this. Nearly a year ago, in 1888, Rev. Tenney preached a thrilling sermon from the above text. The building committee, remembering what a wonderful influence the sermon had, decided it would be a deserved compliment to have their pastors' words put onto a banner and hung onto the walls whose construction of which he gave the first effective start.

In the afternoon of that day, a meeting was held in which Revs. Barkdull and James, of the M.E. and Baptist churches respectively, delivered good addresses and gave words of encouragement. In the evening, Rev. Ferguson of the Marysville Presbyterian church, preached an excellent sermon. Afterward, Mr. John Landon, the energetic chairman of the building committee, read the financial report, from which the following figures were taken:

The amount subscribed by the Presbyterian society of Richwood..$2830

The ladies of the church gathered and paid over a

fund...$444

The Sunday school, Sunday school classes and individuals belonging to the church society gave to the building and its equipment in memoriams and special gifts nearly..$309

  Total..$3574

Besides the contribution in money, the members of the church contributed a large amount of gratuitous labor:

Richwood and vicinity...$615
York church and vicinity..$268
Marysville and friends...$152
Mansfield friends...$75
Mt. Vernon friends...$75
Urbana Friends..$50
Marion Friends...$32
Board of Church Erection...$600

The following is a clipping from the Richwood Gazette that lists the various gifts and furnishings donated to the church by various people:

The following memorials and special gifts were made to the building and its furnishings:

Window, in memoriam of Rev. H. Shedd, D. D., by his sons.

Window, in memoriam of Louisa J. Herron, by Mrs. Rev. John Tenney.

Triple window in memoriam of Mrs. L. R. King, by Chas. King and Dr. E. Y. King.

Triple window, in memoriam of Jas. and S. M. Landon, by Mrs. Jas. Landon, John Landon, Mrs. S. E. Long and E. B. Landon.

Window, special gift, by J. K. and R. Lowe.

Window, special gift, by Mrs. H. E. Conkright's Sunday school class.

Window, special gift, by infant class.

Bailey light, by special contributions and the ladies.

Pulpit, by Rev. John Tenney.

Pulpit suite of chairs, by Sunday school.

Communion set (six pieces) by M. M. Shipley's Sunday school class.

Communion table, by J. L. Horn's class.

A fine 12-lamp chandelier, by Delaware friends.

Pulpit bible, by Master David Ogan.

A handsome clock by a friend.

Pair collection plates, by Mrs. M. M. Shipley.

A beautiful scarf for table in Sunday school room, by Mrs. H. M. Wright, Utica, Nebraska.

Donations given to the Presbyterian Church in 1889. Via Richwood Gazette, January 24, 1889.

The building and lot on which it stands represented a value of $6,000. $241 was raised during the dedication ceremony. This was sufficient enough to cover all unpaid balances so that when the subscriptions were collected (amounting to almost $400), the church was entirely free of debt. Mr. M.M. Shipley and Mr. J.L. Horn did most of the financial work, especially in collecting subscriptions. John Landon managed most aspects of the construction of the building, from the beginning to its completion. He made estimates and contracted for the greater part of the materials and saw that contractors and workers alike kept up their work.

A postcard from 1920 which displays the Richwood Presbyterian Church on the front. The building which housed the church is still standing and is located at 101 E. Blagrove St. Courtesy of Richwood-North Union Public Library. Via Ohio Memory.

The building was constructed by the use of folding doors so that the large Sunday school room can be opened and made into a convenient annex to the auditorium which made the entire seating capacity near 500. The building is made of select brick with a complete heating system, at the time, of a hot air furnace. The windows were made of cathedral glass in bright and elegant colors. The inside wood was made of the most elegant grain of Georgia pine. The plastering was of a gray sand finish. The ends of the pews were of the finest white oak, all finished in hard oil varnish. The floors in all the rooms were covered in the same quality and pattern of wool carpet. The pulpit was made of black walnut upholstered with garnet plush. The suite of chairs at the communion table matched the pulpit in quality and color. Near the pulpit platform sat an Eslesey's church organ. The room was lighted by a Bailey light that filled the entire auditorium with rays of light.

The church congregation had about 80 members by this time. The Richwood Presbyterian congregation dissolved sometime in the

1960s. The building was also the home of the Richwood Church of Christ and served as headquarters for the All-American Quarter Horse Congress for a short time after their previous building had caught fire. The church building still stands to this day, although it now serves as a place of residence.

Chapter 5

WOMEN'S SUFFRAGE IN RICHWOOD

While Women's Suffrage was a country-wide event, the effects of it were widely seen at the local level as well. The 19th Amendment was passed by Congress on June 4, 1919 and ratified on August 18, 1920. The amendment guaranteed the right to vote for women after decades of protest and agitation. And even then, it seemed like it came much later than it should've. The Suffrage Movement was discussed as early as 1848 with the first attempt to organize occurring in Seneca Falls, New York. It was decided that this meeting began the suffrage movement. "The Declaration of Sentiments" was written by Elizabeth Candy Stanton during this time which created an agenda for women's rights. Because of the federal system, the women's right to vote could be achieved via either a federal or state constitutional amendment. However, since the electorate was composed of a mostly hostile white male constituency, there was no hope for women's suffrage.

In 1869, the movement became a national organization known as the National American Woman Suffrage Association (NAWSA), founded by Elizabeth Candy Stanton and Susan B. Anthony, which favored lobbying congress to pass a federal amendment. A more conservative organization called the American Woman Suffrage Association (AWSA) was founded the same year and favored to amend individual state constitutions. It wasn't until around 1910 when the women's suffrage movement, among other reform issues like prohibition, started to move to the forefront of American politics. We see the suffrage movement now as uncontroversial while prohibition became somewhat of a political aberration.

An article that appeared in the Richwood Gazette stating that Dora Sandoe Bachman will give a lecture in Richwood on Oct. 10, 1914. Via Richwood Gazette, Oct. 8, 1914.

The State of Ohio had a lot of early suffrage activity along with two women's rights conventions. At the Ohio Women's Rights Convention in Akron, Sojourner Truth delivered her memorable speech "Ain't I a woman?" Harriet Taylor Upton, mentored by Susan B. Anthony, served as treasurer for NAWSA and as president of Ohio Woman Suffrage Association from 1899 up until 1920. In 1916, Suffragists were certain of Democrat's help and understood that the suffrage movement couldn't win as a partisan issue. In the 1916 presidential election, it was pointed out that Woodrow Wilson, a Democrat, voted for suffrage claiming, "We recommend the extension of the franchise to the women of the country by the States upon the same terms as to men."[10] His opponent Charles E. Hughes, a Republican, did not vote for suffrage and stated that "suffrage is the result of social unrest, that it will cause sex antagonism, and that it raises a disturbance which might as well be stopped."[11]

On October 15, 1914, Mrs. Dora Sandoe Bachman gave a lecture in Richwood in the "public square" on Women's Suffrage. The Richwood Gazette reported that, "Mrs. Backman is a prominent Columbus woman, being vice president of the school board of that city. She is considered the foremost suffragette speaker in Ohio. A good crowd of people gathered around the band stand, from which she spoke and many of the thoughts expressed by her were echoed in the minds of the listeners. Mrs. Bachman's arguments were sensible and showed the plausibility of her side of the question. She was here under the auspices of the local W.C.T.U. of which Mrs. E.A. Schambs is chairman. Mrs. Bachman was introduced by C.E. Kagay, an old school mate. She is a practicing lawyer in the Capital City. A conservative estimate of the number gathered around the platform is between 500 and 600. This is the largest crowd attracted by a political speech here for some time."[12]

Ohio had, at least twice, attempted to pass a Women's Suffrage measure in Ohio's Constitution. The first attempt was held at the 1912 state election. Citizens of Richwood and the state of Ohio voted on a total of 42 different amendments. They adopted various initiatives and referendums including judicial reform, municipal home rule, minimum wage, eight-hour public work day, compulsory primaries, and the abolishment of prison contract labor. 34 of the amendments passed while 8 of them did not. The ones that didn't pass included Amendment 2: the abolishment of capital punishment (death penalty), Amendment 23: gives women the right to vote, Amendment 24: deletes the word "white" from voter qualifications, Amendment 25: allows the use of voting machines and Amendment 36: allows women to hold certain offices. The Richwood Gazette headlined the election results as saying, "Early Returns Indicate That Ohio Will Have One of the Most Radical of Constitutions."[13] Amendment 23 was defeated with 57.46% of the vote.

The second attempt occurred in the Ohio 1914 ballot measure. There were only four constitutional amendments appearing on the ballot. Amendment 1 provided home rule on alcohol and was the only amendment to pass. Amendment 3 would have provided women the right to vote in Ohio. However, it was defeated with 60.71% of the vote, a 3.25% increase since the 1912 election.

The March for Suffrage parade happened in Cleveland, Ohio on October 3, 1914. More than 10,000 women marched down Euclid Avenue for the cause of woman suffrage. Many of them carried signs that read "Votes for Women" and wore modest, ankle-length dresses. The march was to promote the Ohio Women's Suffrage Amendment which appeared on the November 1914 ballot. The measure would have given voting rights to women, but it was defeated by 180,000 votes.

The Reynolds' presidential suffrage bill was passed by the Ohio senate on February 21, 1917 by a vote of 19 to 17 and followed the house, 20 to 16, in passing the bill. The bill allowed women voters to vote in presidential elections. A presidential election wouldn't happen in Ohio until November of 1920. Three Republican senators voted nay— Harding, O'Brien, and Shohl. The other eight Republicans voted for it. 14 Democratic senators voted against the bill and 11 voted for it. The bill was signed by Governor Cox and was to be included on the ballot in November of 1917 for voters to decide if this veto referendum was to pass.

The Richwood Gazette reported that the 1917 election brought out a large vote in Richwood, although no one seemed to show much enthusiasm. The rural vote in Claibourne Township was heavy as the farmers came in during the late afternoon in large numbers. Reports indicated that while Ohio did adopt a state-wide prohibition on alcohol (which was also on the ballot), the suffrage referendum which would have allowed women to vote in presidential elections was defeated with 57.37% of the vote. In the Richwood Village, the results for the referendum were 251 for, 222 against. In Claibourne Township, the results were 155 for, and 111 against. Despite local support, the referendum did not pass state-wide.

It wasn't until the 19th Amendment was ratified on August 18, 1920 that Women in Ohio were finally allowed the right to vote. Curiously, the Richwood Gazette only mentioned the passing of the 19th Amendment on the second to last page of their Aug 19, 1920 issue. Even then, they only included a short article written by the Toledo Blade acknowledging the work that suffrage movements went through to pass the amendment. After the federal constitution was amended in 1920 to give women the right to vote, Ohio voters approved Amendment 2 in 1923. It eliminated the phrase "white male" from the Ohio Constitution in order to provide universal suffrage and conform with the U.S. Constitution.

Chapter 6

RICHWOOD LIBRARY ASSOCIATION

The Richwood Public Library as we know it was formed on January 26, 1915 with the organization of the first library board. However, you may not know that Richwood had an association library in 1882. On June 19, 1882, a meeting was called at the Methodist Episcopal Church to discuss the formation of a "library club." A number of people met and the following minutes of the meeting were furnished by the secretary:

"The Richwood Library Association met to organize. A.J. Blake was called to the chair; P.R. Mills, Secretary. Constitution presented and considered, article by article, and adopted. Rules governing the Librarian were adopted. The Association went into the election of officers, resulting as follows:

President– A.J. Blake, Vice President– Mrs. Lizzie King, Secretary– P.R. Mills, Treasurer– G.B. Hamilton, Librarian– Robert Smith.

P.R. Mills and J.D. Slemmons were appointed a committee to solicit payment of membership fee. On motion, a committee of five was appointed to assist the President in selecting books for the library. Following is the committee: P.R. Mills, A. Watson, J.P.

Brookins, J.D. Slemmons, Robert Smith. Adjourned to regular meeting or to call of Secretary."[14]

The constitution of this Association is as follows:

Article 1. This society shall be known as the Richwood and Vicinity Library Association.

Article 2. The object of the Association shall be to promote the mental and moral culture of its members.

Article 3. Those who have purchased shares in the Richwood Library, or who may hereafter pay the amount of $3 shall become members of the Association.

Article 4. The officers of the Association shall consist of a President, Vice President, Secretary, Treasurer, and Librarian, who, together, shall constitute a Board of Managers.

Article 5. It shall be the duty of the Board of Managers to solicit new members, select the books that may be added to the library, and have general supervision over the business of the Association.

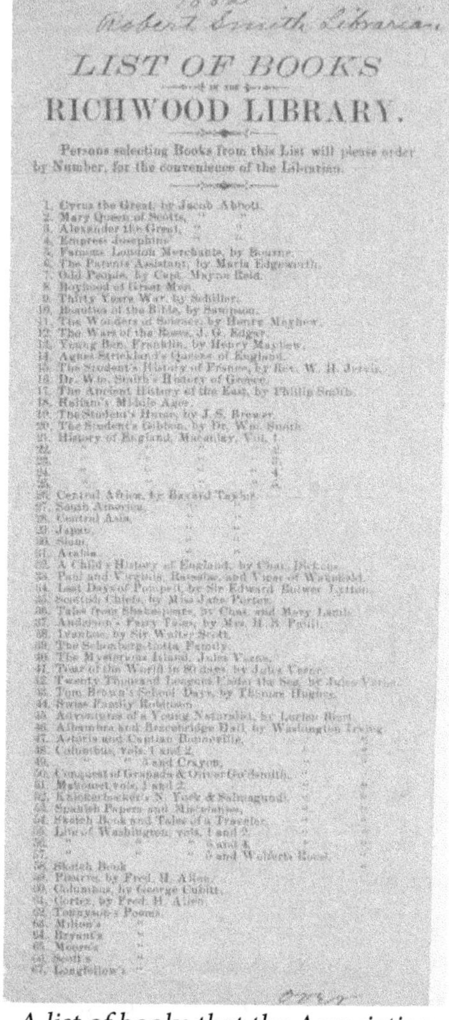

A list of books that the Association owned in 1882. The books included classics such as "A Child's History of England" by Charles Dickens, "Twenty Thousand Leagues Under the Sea" by Jules Verne, and "Last Days of Pompeii" by Sir Edward Bulwer Lytton. Courtesy of Richwood-North Union Public Library. Via Ohio Memory.

Article 6. The Secretary shall keep a record of the proceedings of each meeting, a list of the names of members, and give due notice of the time and place of holding all meetings.

Article 7. The Librarian shall have charge of the books, and be responsible in caring for the same. He shall keep a separate account with each member drawing books in a register provided for that purpose. He shall collect all fines and enforce strictly the rules of the Association. He shall also, at each meeting, report the number of volumes taken out during the term, and the general condition of the library.

Article 8. The annual meeting of the Association shall be held on the 1st Friday of September in each year, at which time the officers shall be elected. The semi-annual meetings shall be held on the 1st Friday of March, in each year.

Article 9. On the request of five members, the Secretary shall call special meetings, but the object of such meetings must be stated in a published notice.

Article 10. Ten members shall constitute a quorum for the transaction of business.

Article 11. The officers shall be elected by ballot, unless otherwise determined by the Association. Members are entitled to one vote for each share they hold.

Article 12. Members may transfer their shares to other parties, by giving notice to the Secretary and Librarian.

Article 13. No alteration or amendment of this Constitution shall be made, except at an annual or semi-annual meeting, and by consent of a majority of the members.

The following rules of the Association include:

1. Members are allowed to take from the library two volumes at a time, for each share they may hold.

2. Books may be retained two weeks, and be renewed for the same period.

3. No person shall be permitted to lend a Library book to

another person not a member of the same household.

4. Any member who shall retain a volume longer than the rules permit, shall be fined two cents per day for such unlawful detention.

5. All injuries to any book beyond a reasonable wear shall be made good to the satisfaction of the Librarian, by the party liable therefor.

6. All books lost or destroyed shall be paid for by the member losing or destroying the same.

7. Members shall not be permitted to take books from the library, or transfer their shares, while any fine against them remains unsettled.

Robert Smith served as Librarian for the Library Association and also served as the chief editor and publisher for the Richwood Gazette. He later served two terms as treasurer for Richwood and two terms as treasurer of Union County. Afterward, he purchased the Marion Transcript newspaper, which changed its name to the Marion Republican. After about a year, he sold the Marion Republican and bought the LaRue News which he edited for about a year before moving back to Richwood and engaged in the fire insurance business.

His health became an issue which prompted him

A portrait photo of Robert Smith appearing in the RIchwood Gazette. Via Richwood Gazette, Sept. 16, 1909.

to quit this business and served as a rural mail carrier on route 5 out of Richwood. He was married to Miss Minnie Beem on Thanksgiving Day in 1884 until Thanksgiving of 1907 when Minnie passed away due to breast cancer. After her death, he always seemed to be exceedingly sad and rarely left his residence. He devoted most of his time taking care of his sister who stayed with him. Mr. Smith had suffered a stroke of paralysis and passed away on September 12, 1909 at 55 years of age.

Reportedly eighty people had subscribed to the Association at one point. A membership fee of $3.00 was required to join; of which amount $2.50 was expended for the purchase of new books and book cases, and the additional 50 cents allowed for their share of the incidental expenses. It is unknown how long the Association lasted before an official public library was finally established in 1915.

Chapter 7

RICHWOOD HOME COMING WEEK

In the Richwood Gazette on July 21, 1910, "On the 8th day of August, 1832, Thomas G. Plummer, a special deputy surveyor under the direction of Levi Phelps, surveyor of Union County, made the survey of the town site of Richwood, which as that time was in the midst of a dense wilderness. What date could be more appropriate for a Richwood Home Coming than the first week in August 1910, the seventy-eighth anniversary of our town?"[15]

This article came from the Richwood Gazette on July 21, 1910. The thought was that the five hundred or so families, who at some point during those 78 years had changed their address, would perhaps wish to visit their old associates and acquaintances in and around Richwood. Flags and banners were strung everywhere in town to welcome visitors. During the week, there were various displays including one in the mayor's office which held many curiosities of pioneer days such as photographs of the early settlers of Richwood, scenes about Richwood in pioneer days, and many other things. The fair was also in session during Home Coming week which included a balloon race and parachute drop, a concert of the Fourth Regiment Military Band, and of course 4 horse races on the "best half-mile track in the state."

The Richwood Gazette reported that over 600 people came to Richwood during the Home Coming Week. One of the biggest attractions that occurred was a high wire performance by James E. Hardy. He gave a show each day and was greeted by a large crowd each time he attempted his miraculous feats in the air. Tuesday morning, August 2, 1910, at promptly 6:30 before many citizens of Richwood were up ad about, all the whistles were blown, accompanied by the ringing of the church bells and firing of anvils, for ten minutes, formally opening Home Coming week.

The entertainment on Wednesday included a baseball game between the Home Comers and the New Comers, the outcome being 9 to 8 with the old "has beens" defeating the younger fellows by one point. This day also included a trip to the Richwood Fair and the reunion of the old comrades of Company G, 14th regiment O.N.G. and the old 14th regiment band.

Thursday morning witnessed a reunion of the old students and high school alumni at the school building. Reportedly quite a large number of former

The cover of the official Home Coming Week program book. Courtesy of Richwood-North Union Public Library. Via Ohio Memory.

teachers and students were present.

The program committee had prepared quite a surprise for everybody in the shape of a picture show for Thursday evening. Photographs of many of the older residents of the town, a few of whom were still living, had been obtained and slides were made from them. The pictures were shown on a screen on the building that was occupied by the Farmers Deposit Bank. The street opposite was jammed with people pushing and scrambling to get as close as possible. Proceeding the show was a sextette composed of J.A. Phillips, S.A. McNeil, Don Van Winkle, C.G. Johnson, Dr. Brown and Fred Rapp, sang the following official song of the Home Comers:

My Old Richwood Home
Tune, "We'll Stand by the Colors" by J.A. Phillips.
[ALL JOIN IN THE CHORUS]
Where a village stands in splendor
In the grand old Buckeye state,
There the welcomes, warm and tender,
For my wandering footsteps wait.
'Tis the place where hills in glory
Sparkle 'neath the morning's beams.
'Tis the land of song and story,
And the palace of my dreams.
Chorus
Home, sweet home, my dear old Richwood home.
Back where the roses and the wild clematis bloom,
Home, sweet home, I'm going home once more,
Back where the voices of my loved ones bid me come.
I can hear the robins singing
As they sang in days before,
'Mid the morning glories clinging
To the trellis by the door.
I can hear light footsteps falling

When the evening breezes blow,
I can hear loved voices calling
From the days of long ago.
How we linger and we listen
When the dear old song is heard.
How the eyes will dim and glisten
As we harken to each word,
And with happy visions thronging
How we join the sweet refrain,
Till our hearts are filled with longing
For the dear old home again.

The Richwood Gazette includes a list of names of those whose pictures were shown during the show. A few names include: Dr. John P Brookins, Grandma Brookins, Andrew McNeil, Jacob C. Sidle, Judge Hastings, Uncle Peter Finch, Orrin Beem, Dr. E.Y. King, and Mr. and Mrs. William H. Conkright.

A drawn rendering of visitors coming to Richwood Home Coming week on the Columbus, Magnetic Springs and Northern electric line. Via Richwood Gazette, Jul. 21, 1910.

The grand mardi gras festival on Friday evening concluded the week's program and was joined in by both young and old, and dozens of amusing costumes were present. C.J. Fifer, manager of the C.M.S. & N. railway, had the company's work car furnished with seats and decorated in flashy colors. Along each side of the car was stretched a large banner bearing the words, "C.M.S. & N. Summer Car," and needless to say the car was packed with jolly masqueraders and amusing costumes with each trip it made through town. The following prizes were given for the best costumes:

Best Uncle Sam, box cigars given by Bruce Street Grocery- won by C.J. Fifer. Hazel Osborn was the best masked lady, and received a pair of kid gloves from the Robinson & Wilkins Co. For the best masked gent, the Peet Hardware Co. offered a pocket knife; the judges awarded this prize to Harry E. Peet of the above-named firm. Miss Helen McAllister received the China salad dishware given by J.W. Kyle & Son for the best Spanish dancing girl. The Roman chair offered by F.L. Winter for the best Indian costume was won by J.G. Smith. George W. Worden was awarded the necktie given by A.I. Glick for the best comic gent. The $2 worth of bathroom essentials offered by M.C. Wolgamot for the best Indian maiden was awarded to Miss Ruby LaDow.

Chapter 8

VARUNA PARK: THE GOD OF WATERS

While Magnetic Springs was famous for its healing mineral water, Richwood was no stranger to these discoveries. Mineral water was thought to provide many benefits. By the 19th century, thermal resorts had become fashionable destinations for those who wished to bathe and enjoy the therapeutic benefits of mineral water. Many hoped to find miracle cures for their ailments.

The C.D. Sidle farm in Richwood was located slightly west of the fairgrounds. In 1899, the Richwood Oil, Gas, and Mineral Company, of which a man named J.L. Horn was president, awarded a contract to an experienced driller from Lima, Ohio for the drilling of two test oil wells on the land of Mr. Sidle. Under the terms of the agreement, the contract price for the drilling of the first well was 95 cents per foot until the hole was 100 feet provided oil or gas was not found. If none was discovered, the drilling would continue until the company wishes to stop and the contractor would be paid $1.25 for each foot drilled. While oil or gas was never found, something else entirely was discovered.

On September 19, 1899, the oil well reached a depth of 1652 feet when a vein of mineral water was struck. Dr. L.L. Roebuck was sent to Columbus with a sample of the water to have it analyzed. He went directly to Curtis C. Howard who was a professor of chemistry at the Starling Medical College. Howard said the water was strongly charged with minerals and began analyzing it straight away. Although quite a number of people were disappointed that no oil was found, the board of directors admitted that if it is indeed mineral water, it would be worth more money than an oil or gas well. A few days after the drilling, the water raised in the well to a depth of 1200 feet and it may have eventually overflowed.

At the oil drilling meeting held at the mayor's office on the 26th of September, 1899, a large list of shareholders was present and it was decided to drill another well. The shareholders were required to pay in the last half of their assessment no later than Oct. 7 of that year. As soon as sufficient funds were raised, a contract would be made for the drilling of the second well. The analysis of the water had not yet been received by Prof. Howard at the time. However, in a letter that the professor wrote to Dr. Roebuck a few days prior, he mentioned that the water contained valuable medicinal properties and requested that the doctor wait until a thorough chemical test could be made.

A few days later, the results had finally arrived of a thorough quantitative analysis of the water from Richwood's abandoned oil well. He submitted the result of his investigations to the directors of the Richwood Oil, Gas, and Mineral Company in the following letter:

GENTLEMEN: - The sample of deep well water received from you gives on analysis the following figures:

Sodium Sulphate..145.2
Sodium Chloride..1465.1
Calcium Chloride..80.6
Calcium Bicarbonate..77.3
Magnesium Bicarbonate..80.9
Aluminum Sulphate..21.6

1870.7

Sulphuretted Hydrogen..24.3 cubic inches.
Yours Truly,
Curtis C. Howard

In transmitting his report, Professor Howard said: "The water contains a considerable amount of sodium chloride present. The calcium chloride is also considerable and the aluminum sulphate is unusually high. The water certainly possesses a sufficiently large amount of mineral constituents to entitle it to be called mineral water." Professor Howard's area of expertise was of course to simply determine the chemical composition of the water and it was not a part of his duty to express an opinion as to its medical value. The proportion of sulphuretted hydrogen in this water, as compared with other sulpher waters, is shown in the following table:

Sulphuretted hydrogen gas in cubic inches per U.S. gal.
Weilbach Well, Germany..1.161
Cave Well, Chittenago, N.Y..2.754
White Sulphur Well, Chittenago, N.Y...................................0.884
Florida Well, Montgomery Co., N.Y.....................................3.765
Odevene Spring, Delaware, Ohio...2.924
Richwood Well, Richwood, Ohio..24.3

The Odevene spring of Delaware is still located on Ohio Wesleyan University's campus. The sulphur spring well, which has since dried up, has been turned into a well-known gathering spot for students and faculty. The well only contained 2.9 cubic inches of sulphuretted hydrogen per gallon, while the water from the Richwood well contained over eight times as much of this gas, which was one of its most valuable properties.

In October of 1899, the drilling commenced on the second well on William Biddle's farm located near the first well west of Richwood. As expected, it too proved to be a "dry" hole after drilling 1,500 feet and was promptly abandoned. Mr. and Mrs. Biddle entertained the four men on the drilling crew at their home when the drilling was complete. Three of the men were Welsh along with Mrs. Biddle who was of Welsh parentage. The evening was spent in the singing of Welsh songs with Mr. Jones, captain of the drilling crew, acting as pianist. Oysters and other refreshments were served.

A picnic gathering at Varuna Park circa 1900. Photo courtesy of Chuck Barry.

In December, the Richwood, Oil, Gas and Mineral Company met at the mayor's office once more and it was decided to organize a stock company for the development of well number 1 on the Sidle farm and put the mineral water on the market. The company was capitalized in the sum of $10,000 and the stock was sold to the members of the Richwood OGM Co. for $10 each as long as any member of the old company wished to do so. After which, it was offered to the rest of the public.

On December 18, 1899, the Varuna Water Company filed their articles of incorporation to the Ohio Secretary of State and began to develop well no. 1 of the old Richwood Oil, Gas, and Mineral Company. The water was named "Varuna" which is a Sanskrit word meaning "the God of Waters." On December 28, 1899, the stockholders of Varuna Water Company met at the private office of the Deposit Bank in Richwood. After some time, a committee consisting of J.B. Miller, J.M. Wilkins, and George W. Worden was appointed to draft the by-laws and constitution. After they were met with approval, the following list of officers were elected: J.L. Horn, president; J.M. Wilkins, vice president; W.H. Wagers, secretary; and Bent Cahill, treasurer.

The Varuna Water Company contracted with a Baltimore firm for a bottling machine which was placed in the building constructed on the land purchased from C.D. Sidle. The Richwood Gazette published the following story: On February 12, 1900, the president of the Varuna Water Company, J.L. Horn, had opened an airtight lid to one of the big tanks filled with the water. Upon doing so, sulphonated hydrogen gas was so strong that it completely overcame him, and he stepped back from the tank and gently laid down on the floor. As he dropped, his hat fell to the first story of the building where his men were working and went upstairs to see what was wrong. They were surprised to see Mr. Horn lying on the floor sleeping as sweetly as a baby. They attempted to awake him, but it was about five minutes before they could do so. When he finally came to, he said he felt as though he had been chloroformed and that he believed he would have slept longer had he been left alone.[16]

Varuna water began to sell at the stores of J.L. Horn and Isaac Miller in Richwood. The bottles were sold for 25 cents per gallon. Anyone with stomach, liver, or kidney pain was suggested to try the water. An advertisement in the Richwood Gazette suggested that "If you have that tired feeling and don't enjoy your food, try Varuna mineral water. It will sharpen up your appetite and make a new man of you."[17]

On April 17, 1900, the Varuna Water Company made a big shipment of mineral water to their agent, J.W. Thew, at Marion. It was later said that J.B. Miller made arrangements to sell the water in Columbus.

Varuna Mineral Water

Is the strongest, best and purest mineral water obtained from any well in the state of Ohio. Its medical properties, which may be seen below, compare favorably with any mineral water found in the United States and will, in time prove a blessing to humanity. Read the description of the well, the analysis and testimonials and then give in a trial if you are in poor health.

LOCATION OF VARUNA WELLS.

THE Varuna Mineral Waters are obtained from the Varuna Wells at Richwood, Union County, Ohio, on the Cincinnati branch of the Erie R. R. Richwood has a population of 2000, and on account of its wide streets, stone sidewalks and beautiful shade trees is considered one of the prettiest villages in Ohio.

The Varuna Waters were discovered in September, 1899, in a beautiful grove convenient to the leading hotels and boarding houses. This entire grove of thirteen acres has been purchased by The Varuna Water Co. Bottling works have been erected and it is the purpose of the Company to erect bath houses and further improve the place as a park and health resort. The wells are designated as Well No. 1, (1662 ft.) and Well No. 2, (120 ft.), flowing. All references are to Well No. 1, unless otherwise noted. Varuna No. 1 has wonderful therapeutic properties, and No. 2 is an unrivaled club and table water.

MEDICAL PROPERTIES.

Varuna Mineral Water, as its analysis indicates, is a medicinal agent of rare value; and will of a certainty relieve the following conditions: Dyspepsia, Indigestion, Catarrh of the Stomach and Bowels, Constipation and Flatulency, also diseases of the Kidneys and Bladder by neutralizing the hyperacidity of the urine and relieving Cystitis and Catarrh of the Bladder. When applied locally it will relieve Eczema and all chronic skin affections.

DIRECTIONS FOR USING.

For Indigestion and Flatulency take a wine glass full of the water after each meal. As a laxative take a wine glass full in hot water morning and evening. For all affections of the Kidneys and Bladder, Rheumatism, Etc., it should be taken three or four times a day, well diluted.

CHEMICAL ANALYSIS OF VARUNA.

WELL NO. 1.

	Grains per U. S gallon.
Sodium Sulphate	145.2
Sodium Chloride	1465.1
Calcium Chloride	80.6
Calcium Bicarbonate	77.3
Magnesium Bicarbonate	80.9
Aluminum Sulphate	21.6
	1870.7

Sulphuretted Hydrogen ___ 24.3 cu. inches.

Analysis by PROF. CURTIS C. HOWARD, Starling Medical College, Columbus, O.

WELL NO. 2.

	Grains per U. S. gallon.
Silica	.61
Sulphate of Strontia	2.22
Carbonate of Iron	.25
Chloride of Sodium	1.29
Sulphate of Potassium	.62
Carbonate of Lithium	Trace
Sulphate of Sodium	2.84
Sulphate of Lime	23.42
Carbonate of Lime	5.16
Carbonate of Magnesia	10.65
	46.96

Sulphuretted Hydrogen ___ Traces

Analysis by PROF. N. W. LORD, Ohio State University, Columbus, O.

TESTIMONIALS.

READ WHAT VARUNA WATER HAS ALREADY DONE FOR HUMANITY.

New Confidence in Varuna.

RICHWOOD, OHIO, Feb. 19, 1900.

The Varuna Water Co.,
Richwood, Ohio.

GENTLEMEN:—I have been affected with Rheumatism, Kidney and Stomach troubles for several years and have suffered almost continuously, with pains in my back and stomach. About a year ago I was confined to my bed for over a month, and did not expect to recover. With good medical attendance I gradually became better and was able to be out again, but my trouble was not cured, and a short time ago I felt it coming on again. I commenced taking Varuna Water. I have only used Varuna for about ten days but already feel so much better than I recommend your water to any one afflicted with Rheumatism or Stomach or Kidney trouble. I feel confident that Varuna Water will permanently cure me.

Respectfully,
M. EVANS.

Varuna Greatly Helped Her.

RICHWOOD, OHIO, March 7, 1900.

The Varuna Water Co.,
Richwood, Ohio.

GENTLEMEN:—I have been using your Varuna Water for some time for Stomach and Kidney trouble and it has been of great benefit to me.

MRS. GEO. W. KOONS.

Benefited Her Stomach.

ASHLAND, OHIO, March 7, 1900.

The Varuna Water Co.,
Richwood, Ohio.

GENTLEMEN:—I have been using Varuna Water for Stomach trouble and have been very much benefited by it.

MRS. FLAVIA HALL.

Helped His Stomach.

RICHWOOD, OHIO, Feb. 19, 1900.

The Varuna Water Co.,
Richwood, Ohio.

GENTLEMEN:—I have been using your Varuna Water for stomach trouble and am pleased to say its decreasing symptoms have nearly all been removed. My stomach is stronger, my food digests better and my health and strength have been much improved.

Respectfully,
JAMES W. WILCOX.

Cured Indigestion and Bloating of the Stomach.

RICHWOOD, OHIO, Feb. 19, 1900.

The Varuna Water Co.,
Richwood, Ohio.

GENTLEMEN:—For about two years I have been troubled with indigestion and bloating sensations, with severe pains in the stomach after eating and at night. After taking Varuna Water for about ten days my indigestion has greatly improved and the pains and bloating sensations have entirely ceased. As I have taken no other treatment I cannot attribute the benefit to anything but Varuna Water.

Respectfully,
F. M. WEALEY.

Recommends Varuna as a Wash.

RICHWOOD, OHIO, March 8, 1900.

The Varuna Water Co.,
Richwood, Ohio.

GENTLEMEN:—For a number of years I have been in poor health and was surprised at the improvement in my condition after using Varuna Water. It is wonderful as a wash.

MRS. R. MARTIN.

Cured His Stomach Trouble.

RICHWOOD, OHIO, March 8, 1900.

The Varuna Water Co.,
Richwood, Ohio.

GENTLEMEN:—I have been using Varuna Water for my stomach and bowels and it has effected a thorough cure of my trouble.

Yours truly,
ISAIAH CRANE.

Can Now Eat Anything He Wishes.

RICHWOOD, OHIO, March 1, 1900.

The Varuna Water Co.,
Richwood, Ohio.

GENTLEMEN:—I have had Stomach trouble for about three years. Have been using Varuna Water three weeks and have been much benefited by it. My digestion has greatly improved and I can now eat heartily without experiencing any inconvenience.

JOHN REPASS.

Cured Burning Sensation of the Stomach.

RICHWOOD, OHIO, March 7, 1900.

The Varuna Water Co.,
Richwood, Ohio.

GENTLEMEN:—I have been using Varuna Water for Indigestion and a burning sensation in my stomach. Have used your water three weeks, and am thankful to say that my stomach has given me no trouble since that time. I believe your water is an excellent remedy for stomach trouble and Indigestion.

V. T. BERRY,
Marshal of Richwood.

Cured Sciatic Rheumatism.

RICHWOOD, OHIO, March 2, 1900.

The Varuna Water Co.,
Richwood, Ohio.

GENTLEMEN:—I was confined to my bed for six weeks with Sciatic Rheumatism and Stomach and Bowel trouble. I commenced taking Varuna Water three weeks ago and begin to get better in a few days. I am now able to be up and around the house. I have reason to believe your water has done me much good.

MRS. ELLEN BERRY.

Helped His Stomach and Kidneys.

RICHWOOD, OHIO, March 1, 1900.

The Varuna Water Co.,
Richwood, Ohio.

GENTLEMEN:—I have been using Varuna Water for Stomach and Kidney trouble and find that it is a wonderful remedy for such trouble.

GEO. W. KOONS.

Cured Dandruff With Varuna.

RICHWOOD, OHIO, March 7, 1900.

The Varuna Water Co.,
Richwood, Ohio.

GENTLEMEN:—I have given Varuna Water a trial and find it to be an excellent remedy for dandruff. I was troubled with dandruff and have used your water as a wash for my head with good results.

MRS. J. C. GRAVES.

Varuna Helped Her After Suffering 12 Years.

RICHWOOD, OHIO, Feb. 19, 1900.

The Varuna Water Co.,
Richwood, Ohio.

GENTLEMEN:—The Varuna Water which comes from your wells will certainly be wonderful and long forgotten. I have had stomach trouble for over 12 years, but this water has given me much relief and I believe that it will permanently cure me.

Respectfully,
C. A. LANDON.

TERMS-PRICES.

In Cases.		In Jugs.	
24 Quarts	$5.00	1 Gallon	$ .60
12 Quarts	2.75	2 Gallons	1.20
48 Pints	6.00	3 Gallons	1.75
24 Pints	3.25	5 Gallons	2.50

All prices F. O. B. Richwood.

For cases and bottles returned if freight is prepaid we will allow rebates as follows:

24 Quarts	$1.00	48 Pints	$2.00
12 Quarts	.75	24 Pints	1.00

Prices to the trade will be furnished on application.

THE VARUNA WATER CO.,
Richwood,
Union County, Ohio.

For a short time the proprietors of the wells will sell Varuna to those who call at the wells in person for 25cts. per gallon. Otherwise the above prices will be charged.

A large advertisement which appeared in the Richwood Gazette featuring testimonials and a chemical analysis of the water. Via Richwood Gazette, Apr. 5, 1900.

The Richwood Gazette, in their paper on April 19, 1900, claimed that Austin Rose, of west Ottawa St., was surprised to find a full-grown opossum sunning himself on his front porch. Mr. Rose captured it alive and expected to keep it until next summer and then turn it over to the Varuna Water Company for their zoological garden. This was the only mention of such a garden which may or may not have existed.

In June of 1900, the Varuna Water Company began carbonating the water to make it more pleasant and less "nauseating as it was in its natural state." The carbonating claimed to not destroy its rare medical properties but instead "keeps it pure and makes it sparkle like champagne."[18]

Another large picnic gathering at Varuna Park circa 1910. Photo courtesy of Chuck Barry.

In September 1900, J.L. Horn sold the company over to Isaac Miller. Mr. Miller began extensive improvements, one of which was the creation of a modern bath house. Varuna Park, including the bath house, opened as a pleasure resort at the end of May 1901. The bath house included eight bath rooms, with male and female attendants. Wooden tubs were used for those desiring baths in

Varuna well no. 1 since it was claimed that no other material should be used on account of the properties of the water. In the rooms used by well no. 2, porcelain tubs were used. The park itself was fitted with seats, swings and merry-go-rounds. Refreshments were also served on the grounds. It was reported that over 800 people visited the park on its opening day on May 19, 1901.

In June, Mr. Miller began making arrangements to give band concerts at the park every Sunday afternoon during the summer months beginning on June 29 when Prof. Arens, of LaRue, assisted by the LaRue Cornet Band, opened the season. The public was invited to enjoy the "cool and sparkling mineral water to their hearts' content."[19] No admission to the park was charged.

A new 40-horsepower boiler was purchased for the water plant in July after the old boiler let loose one Sunday morning and blew out one of the heads. Nobody was in the engine room at the time and Mr. Miller was glad that no one was around when the boiler gave out.

A photograph of the bath house at Varuna Park. This image appeared on postcards with some erroneously captioned as being Magnetic Springs. Courtesy of Richwood-North Union Public Library. Via Ohio Memory.

Varuna Park opened for the season on Saturday, June 7, 1902, in the form of a gala day. At 10 o'clock a.m. a grand parade took place in which 100 men on horseback, representing different nationalities, escorted by two brass bands, traversed along the streets of town, and arrived at the park by 11 o'clock. Professional Perry, the high wire wonder, who was famous for juggling, dancing, and riding a bicycle across an ordinary steel wire in midair, was present. Charles G. Parker and "Stump," his educated dog, was also on the grounds. "Stump" climbed a 50-foot ladder and jumped to a net below. This was purported to have been the highest jump ever made by a trained dog at the time. The two brass bands continued to provide music throughout the day. At 3 o'clock, the attractions at the park were moved to Franklin Street in Richwood where programs were rendered during the evening. All jugs and bottles brought by guests were filled with Varuna water, free of charge. Arrangements were made where anyone could secure excursion rates from any point on the Erie railroad.

In November of 1903, Isaac Miller was forced to declare bankruptcy. His liabilities were about $24,000 with assets of about $10,000. He came to Richwood in 1880 and actively engaged in many businesses. He conducted a successful business and owned considerable real estate up until about three years before the bankruptcy, about the time he purchased Varuna Park and made an effort to improve the park and put Varuna water on the market. The sales of the plant since then were not what they should've been and the expenses were very heavy, thereby involving him to such an extent that he was forced to take out money from his other businesses just to keep Varuna Park going. The stock of merchandise formally owned by Mr. Miller was sold in a bankruptcy sale on December 29, 1903. His seventy-two shares of stock in the Varuna Water Co. were sold to Miller's nephew from Cleveland.

The land known as Varuna Park continued to be owned by Isaac Miller. On December 23, 1909, Mr. Miller sold ten acres off the south half of Varuna Park to H.H. Beaner who owned the Sidle farm adjoining the park grounds. On May 25, 1916, Mr. Miller sold the Varuna Park to D.C. and James Cushman of Richwood and Max Meyer of Columbus. They installed a fertilizer plant there named the Richwood Fertilizer Company. D.C. Cushman was manager of the establishment and had full charge of the business. A lawsuit was later brought to the company by a Dr. Bown. It was postponed indefinitely on account of the owners agreeing to cease operations of the plant by April 1, 1918. The suit was brought on to prevent the draining of wastewater from the plant into Fulton Creek and to stop the offensive odors.

Varuna Park had continued to be used as a gathering place for the citizens of Richwood. Many picnics and public sales were still being held on the grounds. The Park

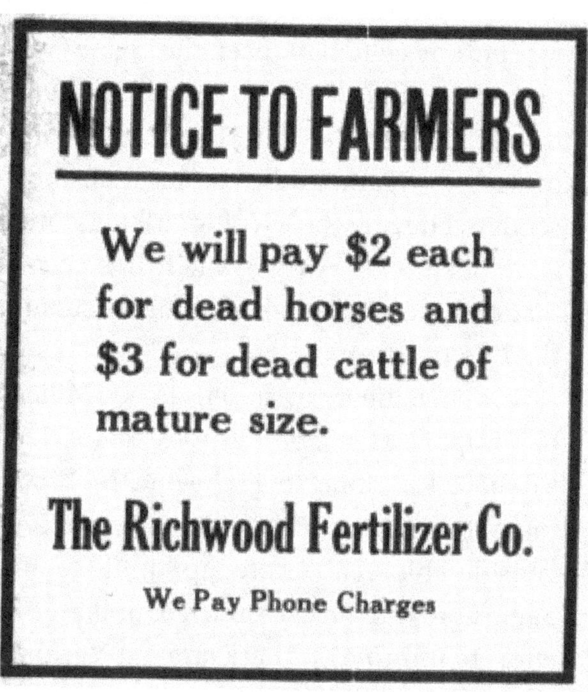

Advertisement of the Richwood Fertilizer Company appearing in the Richwood Gazette, Apr. 26, 1917.

was used until at least the 1930s. After that time, all mention of Varuna Park ceased, and both the park and the mineral water had faded into obscurity.

Chapter 9

OLD RICHWOOD CEMETERY

Most people may not be aware that a cemetery exists on Ottawa street behind what was once the Richwood United Calvary Church. The first person to be buried in the cemetery was Jane Mary Brookins, daughter of J.P. Brookins. The story goes as follows:

"Jane Mary, the little daughter and only child of Dr. and Mrs. Brookins, was playing with her cousins, William and John Woods, and each had a fire. Jane Mary's was burning well, but the boys could not get theirs to burn and asked to make them burn. She took her apron to fan the fire and sat down over some hot coals that had scattered, and her clothing took fire from them. Before help could reach her, she was so badly burned that she died in a few hours."[20]

—A Voice from the Past by W.H. Frank

Philip Plummer, the founder of Richwood, owned the plat and allowed the child to be buried there. He helped clear off the ground and dig the grave for said child. The graveyard grew throughout the years just as Richwood had grown. The cemetery had ceased to be used by around 1860. Some remains were even transferred to the Claibourne cemetery which is now the widely used cemetery in the area. In fact, the Richwood Gazette reported in 1877 how the old lot was full of weeds high enough to hide the tombstones; they implored the Trustees of the township to pay more attention to the place. The burial ground even became a hangout spot for young adults in the town who refused to stay out of trouble.

The tombstone of Jane Mary Brookins located at the Old Richwood Cemetery. The tombstone was last seen leaning against a tree and is not in the same spot where she was originally buried.

The First Baptist Church of Richwood received permission by the Trustees of Claibourne township to lease the lot and build their church in front of the cemetery on Ottawa street for a term of 99 years. The congregation would pay one dollar to the treasury of Claibourne Township with the stipulation that the church keep both the building and the graveyard in good repair and to have a fence constructed to enclose the lots. If at any time the church building shall cease to be used as a house of worship by said Baptist society, then the lot shall become the property of Claibourne township once again.

In 1889, 57 years after Richwood was founded, the heirs of Philip Plummer claimed that since the ground was no longer used for cemetery purposes, it should revert back to the original owner, Philip Plummer. They had brought a suit against the Baptist Church to compel them to pay for the land. The amount they claimed was $200.

On Monday, December 9, 1889, the trial began in the Marysville Courthouse at one o'clock p.m. John Graham was the first witness. He came to Richwood in 1886. He knew Philip Plummer well, and told the court of his good ways but wasn't as specific with times and places and others were. Elder Swartz was the next witness and was well acquainted with the ground on which Richwood

A photo of half of the cemetery. The tombstone leaning against the tree is Jane Mary Brookins. This is one of the only tombstones that still appear legible.

now stands. He was present at the time, in 1832, that Plummer drove into what is now the original town plat and saw them unload the surveyor's tools that were used in laying off the town. In 1838, he (Swartz) heard Plummer say that he would not disturb the graves that had been made on the lots called the graveyard in Richwood; that he had given them to the people, and they had buried on them by his permission and should not be disturbed. He also told of the first grave that had been dug there, Jane Mary Brookins, and that he had burned his hands in trying to help extinguish the fire.

John A.J. Tonguet next took the stand. His age was 83. He also met Plummer in the woods when he came to lay out the town. His uncle, George Clark, took a contract from Plummer to clear and fence the three acres of land immediately east of Richwood and lying between the Prospect and the Hoskins pikes. Uncle George Clark and Nathaniel and John A.J. Tonguet did the work; and when they were ready to commence to make the fence, Plummer came to help lay out the fence row, and the question was asked if the fence should be on the survey line or not. Plummer responded with, "No; I own the land in both surveys, and I want the fence put on the line of the graveyard and other lots, and let the driveway, or the strip of land between the corporation line on the east and west line of the Bull of Claibourne survey be inside the field and the graveyard lots outside."[21] They then set the stakes for the fence by the stakes of the lots of the town. This was in 1835.

William H. Ferguson came next. He produced a deed from Plummer for two unrelated lots that were turned back to Plummer in 1849 by act of the Legislature, and the facts were set up in the deed. L. Myers came to Richwood in the spring of 1842, and buried his children in the lots. John Phillips was born in Richwood in 1836 and remembered Plummer and the graveyard lots well. Asa Langstaff was a Trustee of Claibourne Township and as such made the lease of the lots to the church. This testimony was most all taken in writing on Monday. The stipulations of which is explained above.

Tuesday morning, the court came and H.C. Hamilton was put on the stand. For an hour or more, he told the story of Richwood and the old settlers to an audience of forty or more, mostly lawyers, who gave the best of attention, and now and then indulged in a smile as some peculiar part came to light. He knew Plummer and all his family. He went to school with the older children and knew the younger ones as well. Plummer left Richwood in 1842, early in the fall. He returned on a visit in 1843, during the Millcrite movement and the Second Great Awakening that never came.

Plummer came back to Richwood as a minister of the Methodist Episcopal church in the fall of 1849 and stayed for two years. The people used the Richwood burying ground when H.C. Hamilton left home, in 1853, and they had to a great extent abandoned the use of it when he returned in 1859. The late Joshua S. Gill got the field east of town and the lots west of the graveyard and fenced them all as one piece of land and used the graveyard lots as a pasture field to connect the field and his house and lots.

The original location of the Richwood First Baptist Church built in front of the Old Richwood Cemetery. The congregation later moved to their current building on the corner of E Ottawa St. and N Clinton St. Photo courtesy of Chuck Barry.

In the spring of 1864, the late William Hamilton bought Gill out. Hamilton did not own the lots and lands long before he sold them to Edward Norris. Norris abandoned the field and laid it off in town lots. From then on, the graveyard was neglected, and it became an immense weed patch up until it was leased to the Baptist church. Under control of the church, the graveyard for a time became a pleasant place to go and look upon.

The following is a transcription of the original lease by

Claibourne township to the Baptist Church:

"This article of agreement made this third day of April A.D. 1882 between the Trustees of Claibourne township, Union County, Ohio of the first parts, and the trustees of the First-Regular Baptist Church of Richwood, Union County, Ohio of the second part, stipulates that the party of the first part- so far as they have the right- do hereby lease the old Richwood burying ground on lots No. 29 and 30 in the Village of Richwood, Ohio to the party of the second part- for the term of ninety nine years as a site upon which to erect a church building to be used as a house of worship by said church society.

The party of the second part bind themselves to fulfill the following:

To pay one dollar in money into the Treasury of Claibourne Township and the further consideration of building and keeping in repair a good and substantial fence enclosing said lots. And to at all times keep said lots in such condition that they, the lots, shall be a credit to all parties interested in the same. To the above the party of the second part bind their successors in office; and if at any time the said church building shall cease to be used as a house of worship by said Baptist society, then the same shall become the property of Claibourne township absolutely the same as though it had been built and occupied by said township from the first."[22]

The case was decided that since Philip Plummer had dedicated the lots to a burying ground, those claiming through and under him since his death are stopped from asserting any claim to the possession of said premises. The church was allowed to continue to hold possession of the lots.

As years went by and membership grew, the First Baptist Church built a new building further up the street on the corner of East Ottawa Street and North Clinton Street. The new church was dedicated in 1921. Since their move, the graveyard has largely remained abandoned once more. The original church building was recently purchased as a place of residence and the upkeep on the graveyard lots has since reverted back to Claibourne Township. A few attempts have been made to occasionally clean up the graveyard, the most recent attempt by a local boy scout in 2010; the project of which helped him receive his Eagle Scout Award. Since then, however, the cemetery has mostly gone into decline once more.

Chapter 10

RICHWOOD FIRES OF 1875 & 1968

Richwood had various fires in several months in 1873 and 1875. One of the largest destructive fires occurred on Friday evening on April 9th, 1875 at about 20 minutes before 10 o'clock. The fire was discovered in a barn at the rear of Westheimer's Dry Goods & Grocery Store on the east side of Franklin Street between Blagrove and Ottawa Streets. The building of Thornhill & Godman, a hardware store located across the alley, also caught on fire and both buildings were consumed. The Methodist Protestant church caught fire as well which, together with the

The hardware store of Thornhill & Godman on the east side of Franklin Street before the fire of 1875. Photo courtesy of Chuck Barry.

woodhouse and stable of Richard M. Irwin, was destroyed despite all efforts to save the buildings. A brick wall also fell against the drug store of Cutler & Curry which displaced the shelves and bottles.

Telegrams were sent to Marion and Urbana that the town was on fire and asking for help. In a little over an hour, the Marion Fire Company was on the way with a hand engine. However, the spread of the fire was halted thanks to several citizens with buckets of water as well as the Richwood Hook and Ladder Company who tore down a frame building belonging to A.J. Blake to prevent the further spread of the blaze. In the rear of the block were wooden structures. A water pump was located near these buildings which was utilized by several citizens, namely Dr. Cutler, Mr. and Mrs. Burgner, and Mr. Pringle. They took turns pumping water despite the handle becoming so hot as to burn their hands. The Doctor's face was later found to have been burnt to a blister. The coming of the hand engine from Marion relieved an exhausted people and the village was secured from further harm.

Aftermath of the 1875 fire on the east side of Franklin Street. The citizens of Richwood stand among the ruins of Thornhill & Godman Hardware Store. Photo courtesy of Chuck Barry.

The fire was discovered in Westheimer's stable and was mainly used for packing eggs and filled with straw and litter. It was undoubtedly believed to have been caused by an incendiary. A man was arrested on suspicion of causing the fire, however the man succeeded in making his escape. The man, named George Faun, was later found and charged with having set the fire. He was tried on April 13, 1875 before L.A. Hedges which resulted in a $500 fine. The loss of the fire had accumulated to over $50,000 in damages.

Although the Village Council previously had looked into establishing a fire department, this destructive fire caused them to push it to completion. A hook and ladder company was organized in May of 1875 composing of around 30 members. A steam engine was also purchased from Silsbee & Company located in Seneca Falls, New York. It was received on June 11th, 1875 and costed around $5,250. A hose cart and 800 feet of hose was also purchased. The fire department was a volunteer organization until 1881 when the Village Council organized three departments; a hook and ladder company which consisted of nine members, a hose company which consisted of nine members, and an engine company which had seven members.

✳✳✳

Another fire that occurred in the business district of Richwood in 1968 was as worst as the 1875 fire. On January 31st, 1968, a fire was discovered at midnight by James Reece, a police officer. Flames were shooting 20 to 25 feet in the air by the time the fire department arrived. Reece noticed a heavy amount of smoke coming from the rear of the Richwood Furniture and Appliance Store. Bob Jerew was reported to have turned in the second alarm.

The fire departments from LaRue, Marysville, Prospect and Leesburg also arrived. The firefighters were hampered in their attempts due to heavy fog and the black smoke coming from the fire. By 2:30 a.m., the pressure in the fire hoses were lessened as the village water tank began to run out of water. The fire trucks laid their lines and by setting up a relay system, was able to use the water from the Richwood Lake five blocks away. Firefighting efforts continued all throughout the night. Miraculously, no one was injured while the fire raged on. The last visiting firemen to leave the scene was the LaRue Department at about 5:30 a.m. The Richwood Fire Department stayed well into the morning, putting out small fire that erupted in the debris from time to time.

The aftermath of the 1968 fire. Pictured is the remains of the Richwood Department Store and upstairs apartments. Photo courtesy of Chuck Barry.

Completely lost in the fire were the buildings owned by H.E. Burnside containing the Richwood Department Store, Richwood Furniture and Appliance, and four upstairs apartments. The Richwood Laundromat, owned by C.F. Gill, was also destroyed. The Swartz Motor Sales and Garage received considerable smoke and water damage. Four people who occupied the apartments were removed from the burning building without injury. The estimate of damages was well over $150,000. The cause of the fire was not determined.

After the debris was removed and the corner lot became for sale, it was purchased by the Richwood Public Library Board of Trustees for $15,000. A new brick building was constructed and opened on May 28, 1974. The new library was five times bigger than their former bank building and costed around $156,000 to build.

Chapter 11

RICHWOOD CIVIC CENTER

Not many people know that the Richwood Civic Center exists and how important it is for the community. Since the non-profit was established, the Civic Center has expanded to include many programs as well as providing housing for low-income senior citizens. The monthly calendar is full of activities to encourage elderly participation. The Civic Center continues to host Euchre games, arts and crafts, line dancing and the famous Kitchen Band which continues to provide motivation, travel and fun for the Center's members. Few villages the size of Richwood can boast about having a facility which does so much to benefit the community's seniors.

Ruth Wilson Woods was born February 12th, 1902 in the small town of Warsaw, Ohio. Warsaw is a small village in Coshocton County situated along the Walhonding River. Ruth grew up with her mother and father, Lavada Almack and John Wilson and her older sister by two years, Mary. She later welcomed three younger sisters and a younger brother into the family. Her younger sisters, Ester, Rachel and Lois were all born around a year apart while her younger brother, George, was born in 1909. Ruth continued to live in

Warsaw throughout her childhood. She later met a man named Wellington Seward Mowery. He was born one township over on December 8th, 1900. The pair got married in Warsaw on June 2, 1920. Ruth was 18 at the time of marriage and Wellington was 20 years old. The couple had six children while living in Warsaw.

An early family portrait of Wellington and Ruth with their first two children, Marguerite (left) and Esther (right). Photo taken circa 1923. Courtesy of Anita Davis.

Because of Wellington being a minister, the family moved periodically to various towns throughout Ohio. The family lived in North Lewisburg, Ohio for about three years. They then moved to Renrock, Ohio before ending up at Richwood, Ohio where Ruth stayed for the remainder of her life. America was soon unexpectedly cast into the Second World War. At the age of 41, Wellington was drafted into the United States Army and served as a military chaplain. Ruth continued to raise her children alone with the help of the older ones. Wellington provided the soldiers with religious and spiritual guidance for a few years until the war came to an end with the destruction of the Nazi regime in 1945.

Upon his return, the couple proceeded to live together until the time when both Ruth and Wellington decided to part ways. As her children grew up and moved out of the household, Ruth lived by herself and continued to stay active within the community. She met a man named Harley H. Woods who owned a local candy store in Richwood. Ruth and Harley decided to get married on October 14, 1954 in Richwood when she was 52 and he was 70.

It wasn't until the 1960s that Ruth spoke of an immediate concern for the senior citizens in the community. She had a meeting with the Reverend John Wager, of First United Methodist Church, to discuss with him how there was a need for a meeting space for the community, and perhaps even lunches served, as well as housing for seniors. Following this meeting, Ruth had an appointment with Doctor W.P. Drake. She spoke to him about the needs of the community's seniors. Being the local physician, Dr. Drake was also aware of many of her concerns. At that time, he was also good friends with Reverend Wagner. Both men had contracted polio when they were young. Dr. Drake mentioned this need to the various businessmen in the community such as other doctors, lawyers and farmers. Many of the town's businessmen and women would gather at the local eatery, Boyd's restaurant, for lunch.

As time went on, enthusiasm for addressing these concerns built. There were very few senior citizen centers in those years. On February 19, 1962, the interested group met at the country home of Dr. Drake. After much discussion on the ways and means, they decided to get started. Several locations were mentioned in Richwood on where to establish the senior center. The Committee of George Keigley, Mayor Lee Kelly, and Charles Adams decided that the Harold Winter building seemed the most suitable at $50 a month. The building was located at 19 North Franklin Street which is still in use today. The local Lions Club paid the first month's rent.

On February 22, 1962, the first committee of the Center met at the Georgie-Porgie Restaurant for a noon luncheon. Temporary officers were elected; Dean Cochran, President, George Keigley,

Vice President and Dr. Drake, Secretary-Treasurer. They also successfully incorporated the Civic Center as a non-profit organization. The Harold Winter building was leased for 5 years and the work began on remodeling. Various materials were donated by the community. They remodeled the front, lowered the ceiling, installed restrooms and new heating systems, and repaired and painted the walls. The local mayor, Lee Kelly, helped to install a new furnace in the building.

The first Civic Center building located at 19 North Franklin Street. Photo courtesy of Anita Davis.

The Center successfully opened its doors to the public on July 2, 1962. Ruth soon had her programs started and going strong. People who wanted to help as hostesses were invited to get in touch with Mrs. Woods. The purpose of the Hostess was to welcome those who came to the Center, help them feel at home and help them to take part in the activities of the Center. Dorothy Stickell, a local writer who published many poems and stories, started a writing class at the Center. Painting classes were also being held with Mabel De Bolt at the helm. The back room was eventually prepared for more classes on how to make various crafts. Ruth put on many programs to both entertain and educate the community.

One of the first money making ideas for the Center was to have an auction with various merchandise donated by the community. On July 21, there was an auction for the benefit of the Center conducted by John Pfarr. Those who had items and wanted to contribute to the Center were asked to get in touch with the committee. A coupon was printed in the Richwood Gazette which could either have been mailed in or given to someone at the Center who would call asking for donations for the auction. The Civic Center stressed that it was open for all and no memberships or charges were required to attend any activities.

On August 16, 1963, Ruth Woods acted as chairman for the purpose of organizing a Golden Age Club. Ruth opened the meeting with an appropriate reading and prayer. Gladys Cheney was elected president by unanimous vote and vice president was given to Ruth Miller. Agnes Drake was voted as secretary and treasurer was A.O. Grooms. The hours of the Center were from noon until 4 p.m. on weekdays. Everyone in town was invited to use the Center room as a place of rest during their lunch hour.

The Center would hold monthly birthday parties where everyone with a birthday in the same month would all celebrate it together. One of the biggest and most important events, however, was the Tetanus Clinics which was first held at the Center on October 20, 1963. The clinics were sponsored by the Civic Center with the active approval and endorsement of all local physicians and the Union County Health Department. It was an effort to provide the community with tetanus protection. A materials fee of fifty cents was asked from all who could pay. Those who couldn't pay received the immunization for free. This was considered the first tetanus vaccination clinic to have been held in the state of Ohio.

A total of 618 persons were immunized against this deadly

One of the "youngest" ladies to receive her tetanus shot was Claudia Brown. She is shown here receiving the inoculation from Miss Evelyn Braun, a member of the Union County Health Dept. Ruth Woods can be seen sitting in the background. Via Richwood Gazette, Oct. 24, 1963.

infection. Four local doctors, five local nurses, and four county nurses were on duty throughout the day. Five weeks later, on November 24, the second dose was scheduled and a third or booster dose was made available a year later in November 1964. This program was a real service to the farm and business people of Richwood and the surrounding area and to many of the elderly citizens who came for their first immunization.

In 1965, the Civic Center hosted a single, yet very large, event that borrowed the best from many different acts. This event hoped to "capture the thrills of a horse race, the action of a Rodeo, the atmosphere of a carnival and the enchantment of an Indian festival. The sum total of all will be found in the Richwood Civic Center Equarnival to be held at the Fairgrounds on June 18 and 19."[23] Championship cattle cutting approved by the National and Ohio Cutting Horse Associations was one of the main attractions for Friday and Saturday evenings. Timed horse contests with all the excitement of a race and the fun of a rodeo were also held that Friday night.

Supplementing Saturday's entertainment was exotic Native

American dances and Princess Beverlee, a 15-year-old television and musical show performer, who presented these various dances. Princess Little Pigeon with her four young warrior sons performed the war dance and Chief Little Fox gave demonstrations in fire eating. White Cloud performed feats with his dart gun and played the drums. Princess Beverlee (of Apache heritage) was the youngest dancer to be named to the Native American Hall of Fame. Many Native American Hobby and Novelty stands featuring various crafts and wares decorated the midway. The carnival atmosphere was created by the presence of the Steinmetz Amusement rides and games and Harold Baker Pony Rides. A Quarter Horse Show featuring halter and performance classes was the main events for Saturday's entertainment.

The Equarnival was sponsored by the Civic Center to further its local civic works. Dr. W. P. Drake himself, put hour upon hour as well as his own money to plan for the Equarnival. The total income from the event was close to $3,700, out of which all bills were paid, and 20 percent of all profit went to the Fair Board for use of the grounds. The Civic Center netted approximately $1,000 for its use at the Center.

Another of the Civic Center's fun ideas was the creation of a troupe that became known as the Kitchen Band. Opal Durnell pushed the piano keys as the other members used various homemade instruments that you can find in your kitchen. Mrs. Goff Zuspan directed the 24-member group as they were invited to several nursing homes to play. Bob Thompson created his own instrument with a broomstick and clothesline. Mr. Buckingham, who at the time was 87 years young, used a drum made from a cookie tin which he beat on with two wooden spoons as drumsticks. Other instruments included a washboard, pie tins, a plastic jug, kazoos, and an eggbeater. Ruth and the other band members decided on wearing aprons and hats as uniforms. The hats were decorated with items from the kitchen. The band won several trophies since they organized in the late 1960s.

Former Ohio Governor, John Gilligan, (third from right) posing with the members of the Kitchen Band after their performance for Flippo's Early Show. Photo courtesy of Anita Davis.

On August 24, 1972, Ruth's daughter, Anita Davis, took the band to Expohio at the Ohio State Fairgrounds. Their performance was a huge success as they gave a thirty-minute concert on stage. A few people who worked for WBNS-TV Channel 10 saw the performance and asked if the band would like to come back the next day to be on Flippo's Early Show. The band members agreed and ordered a charter bus to take them back the next morning. The Ohio Governor, John Gilligan, was in the audience when the band played for the telecast. He posed in a photo with the band members after the performance.

With the assistance of a Federal Grant given by the Ohio Administration on Aging, the Center looked to expand in order to become a multi-purpose service center. The grant became effective on April 1, 1967. The committee of: Dr. W. P. Drake, Chairman; Don Parrott, Dr. Otto Howell and S. Howard Cheney, made several trips to Columbus and did all the paperwork that was necessary. The application included approximately 40 typewritten pages of figures and proposals. In compliance with the application, a special committee was selected as a "Committee for Senior Citizens." As in the past five years, Ruth continued to be Director of the Center.

On September 30, 1970, Ruth Woods was appointed by the Division of Administration on Aging, Ohio Department of Mental Hygiene and Correction to coordinate preliminary activities for the White House Conference on Aging in Union County. These activities were held in September as senior citizens throughout Ohio met for community forums. At the forums, senior citizens discussed their needs and concerns, voted on priorities of these needs and filled out a national questionnaire.

On February 25, 1970, the Board of Directors of the Richwood Civic Center voted unanimously to ask for financing from HUD for a Retirement Housing Project to be located on Grove Street. The project was originally projected to cost over $700,000. The request for the financing of the project was brought before the Richwood Council at a specially called meeting. The body gave their approval to the proposed project. It wasn't until November 10, 1970, when the groundbreaking was held for the $875,000 Richwood Apartments, a retirement project.

A crowd of 65 people along with the North Union local school band were gathered on Grove Street across from the recreation facility at the Richwood Lake. Also on hand for the ceremony were the State Federal Housing Authority, Richwood and Union County leaders and officials, the construction company and architect representatives. A federal housing and urban development grant was awarded the month before. The apartments were built on 10 acres dotted with oak, maple, hickory, and evergreen trees.

State Representative Lloyd George Kerns was the main speaker and commended the people of Richwood for being in the forefront in recognizing the need for this type of housing and doing something about it. Mr. Kerns said that this type of housing will become a necessity more and more with the passage of time, citing statistics on the ever-growing number of older people in the population. John Mullins of Columbus, representing the Galbreath Mortgage Co., acted as master of ceremonies and asked A. O. Grooms, the president of the Richwood Civic Center, to introduce the local people who had taken the most active part in making the development a reality.

Albert O. Grooms, president of Richwood Civic Center, Inc., (second from left) turns the first shovel of dirt to break ground for the proposed $857,000 apartments. Looking from left to right are Rep. Lloyd George Kerns, Richwood Mayor Edward Cowgill and Mrs. Ruth Woods, director of the center. Via Marysville-Journal Tribune, Nov. 10, 1970.

Ruth Woods, the director of the Civic Center, was the first to be recognized since the project started with her instigation. Members of the board of directors were also commended for their part. Others recognized were the first president of the Civic Center, Dr. W.P.

Drake, as well as Don Parrott and George Keigley. Mrs. Ella Wetzel, the assistant director, was also commended for the active part she took in the undertaking.

However, a showpiece home known originally as the Beem House had to be torn down in order to build the apartments. The home was erected in 1883 by Orrin Beem and was to be removed to make way for the new apartment building. Some people fought to move the apartments to another location and floated the idea that the house should stay and be converted into a museum to house pictures, mementos and memorabilia of Richwood. The board gave lack of finances as their reasons for turning down the project and some board members thought that leaving the old home standing would detract from the appearance of the apartment complex. The Richwood Library Board also considered taking over the old home and using it as a library and a historical center, but no decision was reached regarding this proposal.

The Richwood Community Apartments neared completion on July 20, 1971, with the occupancy of some units. There were three basic types of apartments: one-bedroom, two-bedroom and efficiency. Those classified as efficiency contained one room for living, dining and sleeping with separate kitchenette, bathroom, large utility room and walk-in closet. The 63-unit building had 19 efficiency units, 40 one-bedroom and 4 two-bedroom apartments. The activities and services of the Richwood Civic Center moved into larger quarters on the first floor of the building. A large lounge type room was available for club meetings as well as functions as a meeting place for friends and visitors of apartment tenants. This room accommodated approximately 200 people. All Civic Center activities were eventually housed in these areas on the first floor.

After fulfilling her dream of establishing the Civic Center and opening the Richwood Apartments, Ruth decided to retire on March 8, 1973 after eight years as Center director. It was Anita Davis, Ruth's sixth and youngest daughter, to pick up the mantle of responsibility as the new director. Ruth continued to operate the Whip Stitch shop for about five years. The shop, which gets its name from a stitch often used in handwork, was an outlet for the handcrafted items made by the senior citizens of the Richwood Civic Center.

The Civic Center continued with Anita as director for multiple years. She was assisted by her mother Ruth as well as a number of planning committees. The planning committee, chaired by Mrs. Harry George, met early in the spring to set up the schedule for the years program. There was always a waiting list for their trips and sometimes the list got so long that two buses were needed.

On August 28, 1973, Ruth was given the Community Service Award presented by the State of Ohio Department of Mental Health and Mental Retardation Division of the Administration on Aging for her outstanding contributions for the benefit of senior citizens in the Richwood community. Claibourne Grange honored Ruth with the Community Service Award and was presented with a 'This Is Your Life" presentation on all her achievements. The presentation at the beginning of the program featured the honored guest's escort to her place of honor by Claibourne's Worth Master John Ed Bell and County Deputy John R. Bell.

Family members were there to greet her as well as the appearances of the former minister, Rev. John Wagner. Wagner's remarks centered on the early stages and actual organization of the Civic Center and was followed by Dr. W. P. Drake detailing a resume on the money-making projects required to continue the Center in its first location. Mrs. Gladys Cheney next appeared. Her tasks involved the furnishings at the Center and some of the initial organization arrangements. Lastly, Don Parrott related appreciation to Ruth from all senior citizens; citing her introduction into the Central Ohio Senior Citizens Hall of Fame and complimentary remarks on behalf of the Central Ohio Area Agency on Aging and Advisory Council.

Ruth Wood's house located at 22$^{1/2}$ South Franklin Street. The house was demolished in the late 1980s to make room for a car lot for a nearby dealership. Photo courtesy of Chuck Barry.

Ruth continued to live out her life on 22$^{1/2}$ South Franklin Street, which was later demolished, until her death on May 6, 1988 at the age of 86. She unexpectedly passed away of natural causes. She was preceded in death by her husband, Harley Woods, who passed away in May of 1968. Three sisters and one brother also preceded her in death. Her sister, Louis, later passed away on November 22, 1995. Her daughter Esther owned the Union Theatre located inside the Richwood Opera House along with her husband Jerry Anderson from 1934 until 1961.

Anita Davis retired as Director in the early 1980s and was replaced by Jo Ann Wildman. Richwood was fortunate to have so many dedicated individuals who were able to get enough federal money to build a housing complex and an organization that continues to help our community in so many ways.

Chapter 12

OIL DRILLING IN RICHWOOD

As automobiles started to become more popular in the early 20th century, so too did the need for oil. The Texas oil boom started in 1901 that began with the discovery of a large petroleum reserve near Beaumont, Texas. The find was unprecedented in its size and started a rapid industrialization and regional development. While Ohio didn't hold as much oil as Texas, the state was no stranger to oil drilling. In Akron, the Summit Oil Company struck oil at its well in Springfield township on January 22, 1906, at a depth of 2,560 feet. In about five minutes, the pipe filled with oil at a height of 200 feet. A strong gas pressure developed also. The oil well produced about 50 barrels.

Another oil well was struck at North Greenfield a short distance west of West Mansfield in April of 1905. It was tested and proved to be a twenty-five barrel well. Experts predicted that the well would keep getting stronger. J.D. Henson, president of the company running the well, was very pleased with the progress. He immediately put down another well in the vicinity.

In Logan, Ohio, a 1500-barrel oil well was struck on the C.L. Work farm in the Bremen field which stated the wildest oil boom ever experienced in the state of Ohio, not discounting the oil booms of Findlay and Lima. The well came in at midnight on February 27, 1909, and in 45 minutes had filled a 215-barrel tank. Earthen reservoirs were hastily thrown up until the flow could be controlled, which was accomplished after several hours. Before this, the only successful drilling was done in the neighborhood of Bremen and little attention was paid to this end.

Stock in existing oil companies, although only few of them had actually struck oil, rushed skyward and business was practically suspended while investors, large and small, sat surrounded by dozens of pencils and paper, figuring their profits or looking at automobile catalogs. A man who invested $50 in oil stocks weeks or months before the recent oil well discovery found himself possessing a large fortune.

This drawing appeared in the Marysville Journal in 1903. Captioned "Still Watching and Waiting," the Journal explained that work on an oil well east of Marysville was discontinued after drilling 1,650 feet. Via Marysville-Journal Tribune, Mar. 19, 1903.

Varuna Park, the mineral well in Richwood which became popular around 1900, was believed to have had oil underneath. However, even after an attempt at drilling two oil wells, never successfully produced any. Despite this, the Richwood Oil, Gas and Mineral Company was incorporated on January 4, 1909, with a capital stock of $5,000 for the purpose of drilling for oil or gas, as the directors and stockholders saw fit. The man who founded the company, C.S. Grindell, brought expert oil men to investigate the fields around Richwood.

The company was comprised of residents of the vicinity and organized to put men in the field to solicit stock and leases. The leases were taken on regular oil lease blanks, so that everyone would get a square deal. The company expected leases on several thousand acres of land before it began drilling. Three test wells were placed in various places around Richwood. Henry H. Beaver served as president of the company with C.S. Grindell as vice president. Mr. Beaver had considerable experience in such work and had vast property interests in the area, having more than five hundred acres of land which he purchased in the vicinity of Richwood. Some farms were leased by the company by the summer of 1909.

Near Kenton, Ohio, on November 6, 1909, an oil well struck gas at a depth of 1,400 feet which produced about 2,000,000 feet a day. The strike caused much excitement among nearby landowners. The well was found on land leased by a company of Findlay and Ada men who started developing oil fields in northern Hardin County. This well was within twenty miles of the lease held by the Richwood Oil, Gas and Mineral Company and, according to the state geographical reports, was in the gas and oil belt extending through Putnam, Hardin, Union and part of Delaware counties (including Richwood and the vicinity). This certainly encouraged the local company to urge local stockholders to put down a few more test wells.

By April 15th, 1911, the Richwood Oil, Gas and Mineral Co. dissolved. It was believed by many that oil and gas was in the vicinity, but some farmers would not lease because they were frightened by false reports hence the company was crippled. The company's wells and leases were then taken over by another company called the Consumer's Oil and Refining Co. They planned to put down four wells in the territory adjacent to Richwood. Stock was offered at $5 a share. The company owned leases in different sections of the state including the Quincy-DeGraff field, where they had produced oil and gas for several years, as well as leases in Trumbull County.

The last mention of the Consumer's Oil and Refining Co. was in 1913. The company was determined to sell enough stock to justify drilling four wells. Unfortunately, the company was never able to raise enough to drill in the vicinity.

A meeting was held on March 8, 1923 at the Richwood Opera House to discuss testing oil within Richwood once more. The meeting was hosted by Mr. Brackney, who had thirty-five years of experience in the oil fields. He gave a talk on the subject of oil and gas wells. He told his listeners that Richwood is in the oil belt and said the only way to make sure is to drill test wells. Various propositions were placed before Mr. Brackney's plan was unanimously accepted. 400 subscriptions of $25 each needed to be secured to raise enough for three test wells. With around 200 people to accept Mr. Brackney's proposition, 200 more subscribers were needed to continue with the drilling.

Oil drilling began in November in 1923 at the Grindell Farm west of Richwood. Drilling was done by the Community Oil Company, a local company comprised of Richwood stockholders. They drilled a total of 1,993 feet, an additional 150 more feet than planned. Samples were taken to geologists at Ohio State University. The analysis showed no indication of oil or gas.

Another well was drilled on the William Stahl Farm, seven miles north-west of Richwood in January of 1924. By March, not a trace of oil was found in the well and it was plugged and abandoned. The company acquired an oil and gas lease at the Richwood Fairgrounds for a third well. The location was planned in the northwest corner of the grounds, near a previous old well that apparently showed traces of oil 24 years earlier in 1900. There remained a good amount of money in the company treasury but not enough for a third well drilling.

A meeting in May was held for stockholders to decide if more money could be raised or if the third well should be abandoned. While some stockholders didn't want to abandon the third well, not enough capital was raised to continue the drilling. Despite the promises that oil and gas lay beneath the village of Richwood, none has ever been found.

REFERENCES

Prohibition in Richwood

1   Richwood Gazette, September 17, 1908.

2   Richwood Gazette, September 24, 1908.

3   Richwood Gazette, January 28, 1909.

4   Richwood Gazette, April 14, 1910.

5   Richwood Gazette, July 14, 1910.

Halloween in Richwood

6   Richwood Gazette, Oct. 29, 1874.

7   Richwood Gazette. Nov. 5, 1891.

Richwood Presbyterian Church

8   Richwood Gazette, June 24, 1875.

9   Richwood Gazette, January 24, 1889.

Women's Suffrage in Richwood

10   "Wilson's Stand on Votes for Women Contrasted with Hughes' Wabbling." *The Delaware Daily Journal-herald,* November 4, 1916.

11   Ibid.

12   Richwood Gazette, Oct. 15, 1914.

13   Richwood Gazette, Sept. 5, 1912.

Richwood Library Association

14   Richwood Gazette, Jun. 22, 1882.

Richwood Home Coming Week

15   Richwood Gazette, Jul. 21, 1910.

Varuna Park: The God of Waters

16   Richwood Gazette, Feb. 22, 1900.

17   Richwood Gazette, March 1, 1900.

18   Richwood Gazette, June 7, 1900.

19   Richwood Gazette, June 27, 1901.

Old Richwood Cemetery

20   Richwood Gazette, Aug. 12, 1897.

21   Richwood Gazette, Dec. 26, 1889.

22   Union County, Ohio, Civil Court Case Files, Case No. 5667, Journal Volume 15, 1889-1891.

Richwood Civic Center

23   Richwood Gazette, Apr. 22, 1965.